WRECK THIS JOURNAL

TO CREATE IS TO DESTROY

BY KERI SMITH

PARTICULAR
BOOKS

PARTICULAR BOOKS

PUBLISHED BY THE PENGUIN GROUP
PENGUIN BOOKS LTD, 80 STRAND, LONDON WC2R ORL, ENGLAND
PENGUIN GROUP (USA) INC, 375 HUDSON STREET, NEW YORK, NEW YORK 10014, USA PENGUIN GROUP (CANADA), 90 EGLINTON AVENUE EAST, SUITE 700, TORONTO, ONTARIO, CANADA M4P 2Y3
(A DIVISION OF PEARSON PENGUIN CANADA INC.)
PENGUIN IRELAND, 25 ST STEPHEN'S GREEN, DUBLIN 2, IRELAND
(A DIVISION OF PENGUIN BOOKS LTD)
PENGUIN GROUP (AUSTRALIA), 707 COLLINS STREET, MELBOURNE, VICTORIA 3008, AUSTRALIA
(A DIVISION OF PEARSON AUSTRALIA GROUP PTY LTD)
PENGUIN BOOKS INDIA PVT LTD, 11 COMMUNITY CENTRE, PANCHSHEEL PARK, NEW DELHI – 110 017, INDIA
PENGUIN GROUP (NZ), 67 APOLLO DRIVE, ROSEDALE, AUCKLAND 0632, NEW ZEALAND
(A DIVISION OF PEARSON NEW ZEALAND LTD)
PENGUIN BOOKS (SOUTH AFRICA) (PTY) LTD, BLOCK D, ROSEBANK OFFICE PARK, 181 JAN SMUTS AVENUE, PARKTOWN NORTH, GAUTENG 2193, SOUTH AFRICA

PENGUIN BOOKS LTD, REGISTERED OFFICES: 80 STRAND, LONDON WC2R ORL, ENGLAND

WWW.PENGUIN.COM

FIRST PUBLISHED IN THE UNITED STATES OF AMERICA BY PENGUIN GROUP (USA) INC, 2007
FIRST PUBLISHED IN GREAT BRITAIN BY PARTICULAR BOOKS 2010
THIS EXPANDED EDITION PUBLISHED 2013
008

PRINTED IN GREAT BRITAIN BY CLAYS LTD, ST IVES PLC

978-0-141-97614-3

www.greenpenguin.co.uk

MIX
Paper from responsible sources
FSC www.fsc.org FSC™ C018179

Penguin Books is committed to a sustainable future for our business, our readers and our planet. This book is made from Forest Stewardship Council™ certified paper.

WARNING: DURING THE PROCESS OF THIS BOOK YOU WILL GET DIRTY. YOU MAY FIND YOURSELF COVERED IN PAINT, OR ANY OTHER NUMBER OF FOREIGN SUBSTANCES. YOU WILL GET WET. YOU MAY BE ASKED TO DO THINGS YOU QUESTION. YOU MAY GRIEVE FOR THE PERFECT STATE THAT YOU FOUND THE BOOK IN. YOU MAY BEGIN TO SEE CREATIVE DESTRUCTION EVERYWHERE. YOU MAY BEGIN TO LIVE MORE RECKLESSLY.

Acknowledgments This book was made with the help of the following people: my husband, Jefferson Pitcher, who provides constant inspiration for living a full and daring life (some of his ideas ended up here). Thanks to the talented artists Steve Lambert and Cynthia Yardley-Lambert who helped me brainstorm ideas during a lecture on contemporary art. To my editor at Perigee, Meg Leder, who embraced and believed in this project from the beginning, your thoughts and sensitivity left me with so much gratitude. To my agent, Faith Hamlin, for continuing to believe in my artistic/creative vision. Thanks also to Corita Kent, John Cage, Ross Mendes, Brenda Ueland, Bruno Munari, and Charles and Rae Eames, whose ideas and perceptions continue to rip me wide open.

Dedicated to perfectionists all over the world.

THIS BOOK BELONGS TO:

WRITE YOUR NAME IN WHITE.

WRITE YOUR NAME ILLEGIBLY.

WRITE YOUR NAME IN TINY LETTERS.

WRITE YOUR NAME BACKWARD.

WRITE YOUR NAME VERY FAINTLY.

WRITE YOUR NAME USING LARGE LETTERS.

ADDRESS

PHONE NUMBER

* NOTE: IF FOUND, FLIP TO A PAGE RANDOMLY, FOLLOW THE INSTRUCTIONS, THEN RETURN.

INSTRUCTIONS

1. Carry this with you everywhere you go.
2. Follow the instructions on every page.
3. Order is not important.
4. Instructions are open to interpretation.
5. Experiment.
(work against your better judgment.)

materials

ideas
gum
glue
dirt
saliva
water
weather
garbage
plant life
pencil/pen
needle & thread
stamps
stickers
sticky things
sticks
spoons
comb
twist tie
ink
paint
grass
detergent
grease
tears
crayons
smells
hands
string
ball
unpredictability
spontaneity
photos
newspaper
white things
office supplies
wax
found items
stapler
food
tea/coffee
emotions
fears
shoes
matches
biology
scissors
tape
time
happenstance
gumption
sharp things

ADD YOUR OWN PAGE NUMBERS.

STARTING HERE

CRACK THE SPINE.

LEAVE THIS PAGE

BLANK

ON PURPOSE.

STAND HERE.

(WIPE YOUR FEET, JUMP UP AND DOWN.)

POUR, SPILL, drip,
SPIT, fling YOUR COFFEE
HERE.

POKE HOLES IN THIS PAGE USING A PENCIL.

DRAW FAT LINES AND THIN.

PUSHING REALLY HARD WITH THE PENCIL.

THIS PAGE IS FOR HANDPRINTS

OR FINGERPRINTS.

GET THEM DIRTY THEN PRESS DOWN.

COLOR THIS ENTIRE PAGE.

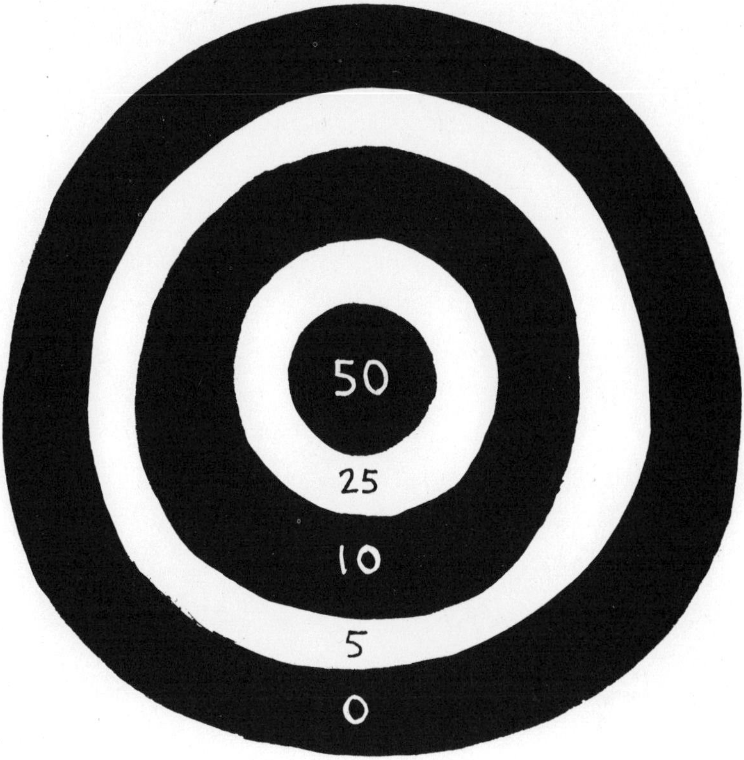

THROW SOMETHING

A PENCIL, A BALL DIPPED IN PAINT.

PRESS LEAVES AND OTHER FOUND THINGS

SCRATCH

USING A SHARP OBJECT.

DO SOME RUBBINGS WITH A PENCIL.

SCRIBBLE WILDLY, VIOLENTLY, *with* RECKLESS ABANDON.

TEAR STRIPS
RIP IT UP!

GLUE,
staple,
OR tape these
PAGES together.

draw lines

ON THE BUS, ON A

While IN MOTION.
TRAIN, WHILE WALKING.

FILL THIS PAGE WITH CIRCLES.

Document your dinner.

RUB, SMEAR, SPLATTER YOUR FOOD.

USE THIS PAGE AS A NAPKIN.

CHEW ON this.

↓

*WARNING: DO NOT SWALLOW.

MAKE A FUNNEL.

DRINK SOME WATER.

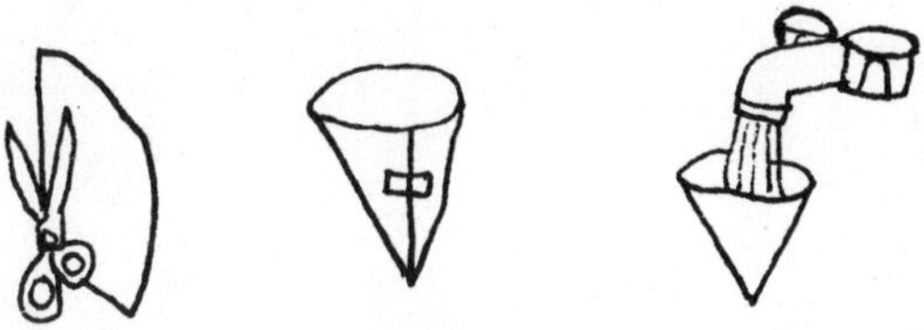

1. CUT OUT.
2. ROLL & TAPE.
3. ADD WATER & DRINK.

TEAR OUT

CRUMPLE.

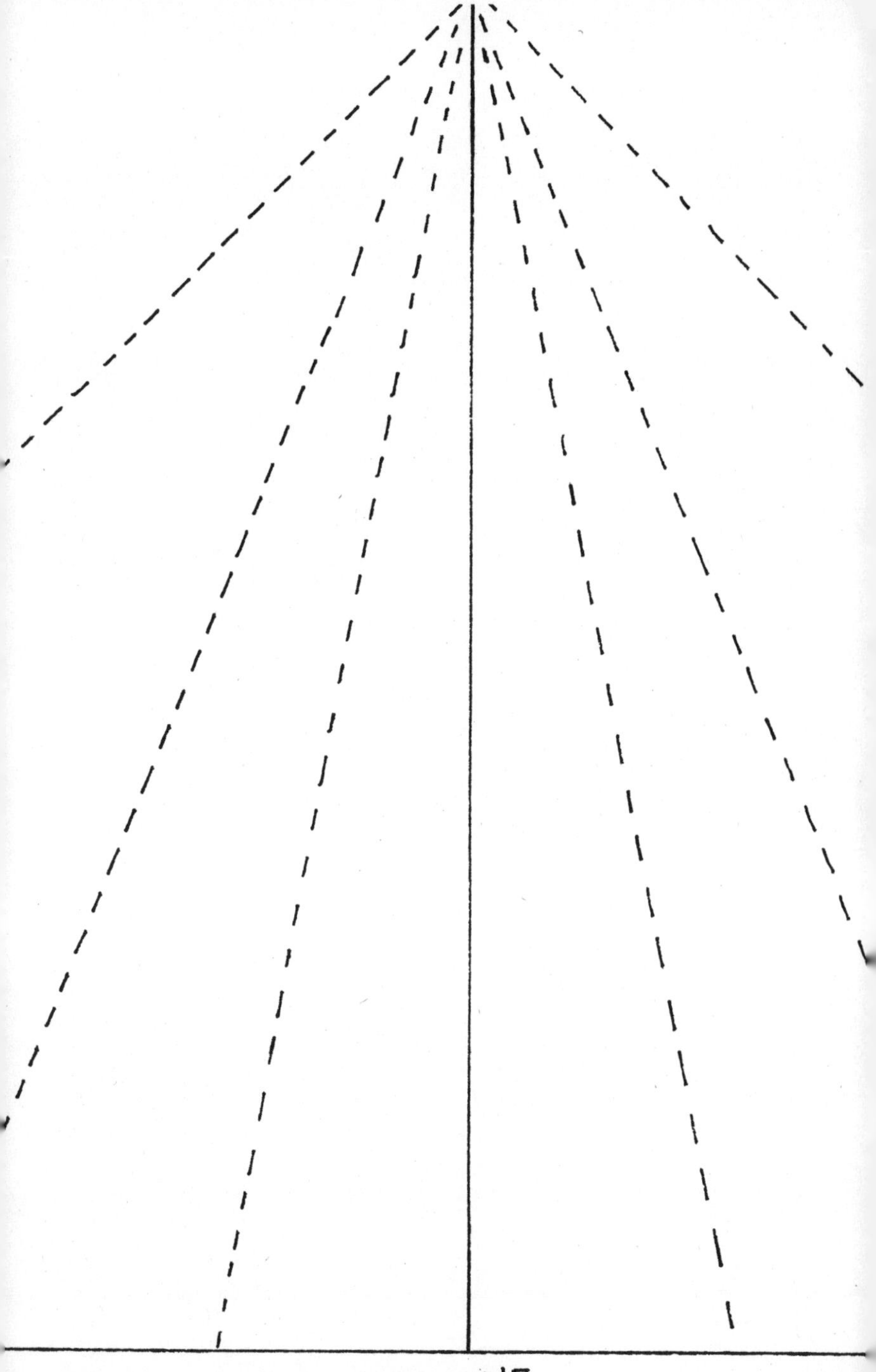

MAKE A PAPER AIRPLANE.

WRAP something

WITH THIS PAGE.

like this

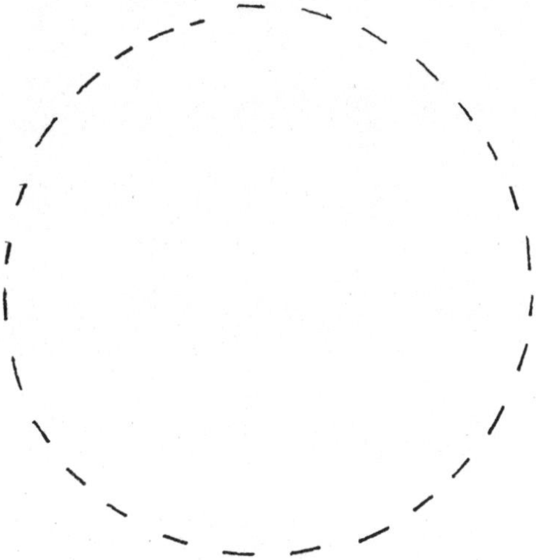

TONGUE PAINTING

1. EAT SOME COLORFUL CANDY.
2. LICK THIS PAGE.

WRITE ONE WORD

OVER AND OVER.

TIE A STRING TO THE *spine* OF THIS BOOK.

SWING WILDLY

LET IT HIT THE WALLS.

PICK UP THE JOURNAL WITHOUT USING YOUR HANDS.

CLIMB UP HIGH

DROP THE JOURNAL.

compost this page.

watch it deteriorate.

DO A *really* UGLY

(USE UGLY SUBJECT MATTER:

A BADLY DRAWN BIRD,

DRAWING 
GUM, POO, DEAD THINGS,
MOLD, BARF, CRUD.)

PLACE STICKY THINGS HERE.
(honey, GUM, syrup, glue, sucker, marshmallow)

PRETEND YOU ARE DOODLING ON THE BACK OF AN ENVELOPE WHILE ON THE PHONE.

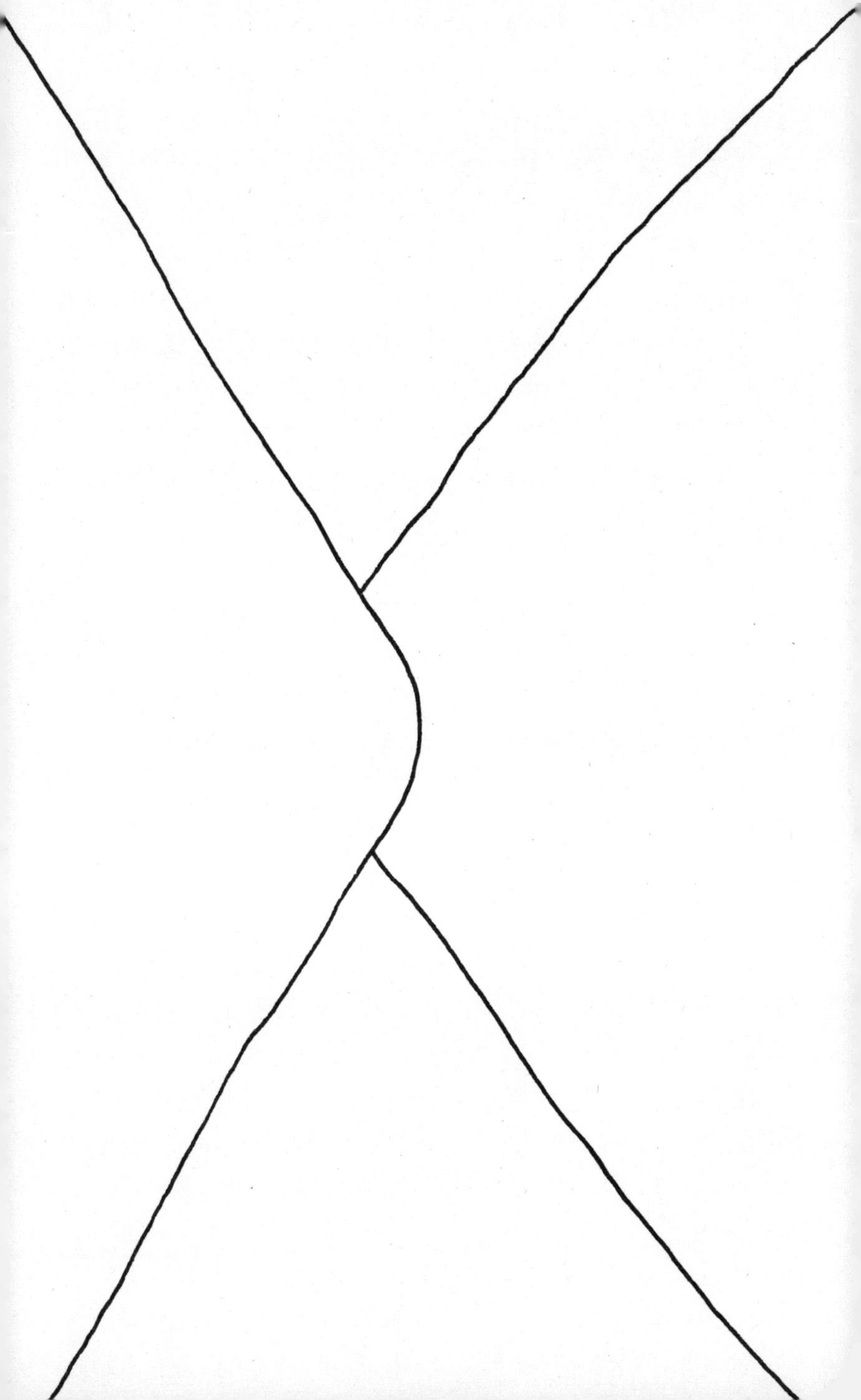

JOURNAL GOLF

1. TEAR OUT PAGE. CRUMPLE INTO A BALL.
2. PLACE JOURNAL INTO A TRIANGLE SHAPE.

3. HIT/KICK THE BALL THROUGH THE TRIANGLE.

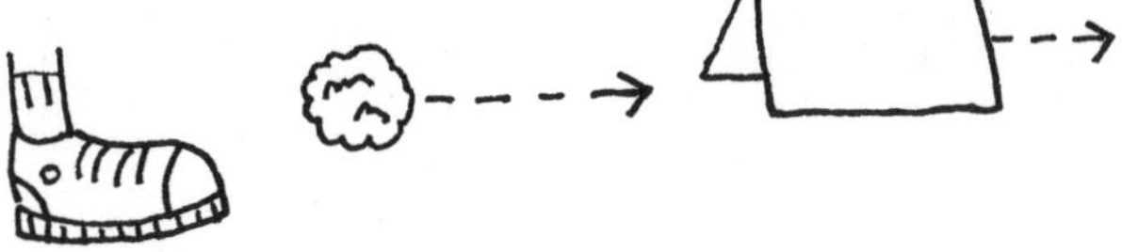

make a paper chain.

COLLECT
FRUIT
STICKERS*
HERE.

* STICKERS YOU FIND ON BOUGHT FRUIT.

COVER THIS PAGE

USING ONLY office SUPPLIES.

BRING THIS BOOK IN THE SHOWER WITH YOU.

TIE A STRING TO THE JOURNAL.

GO FOR A WALK, DRAG IT.

RUB HERE WITH DIRT.

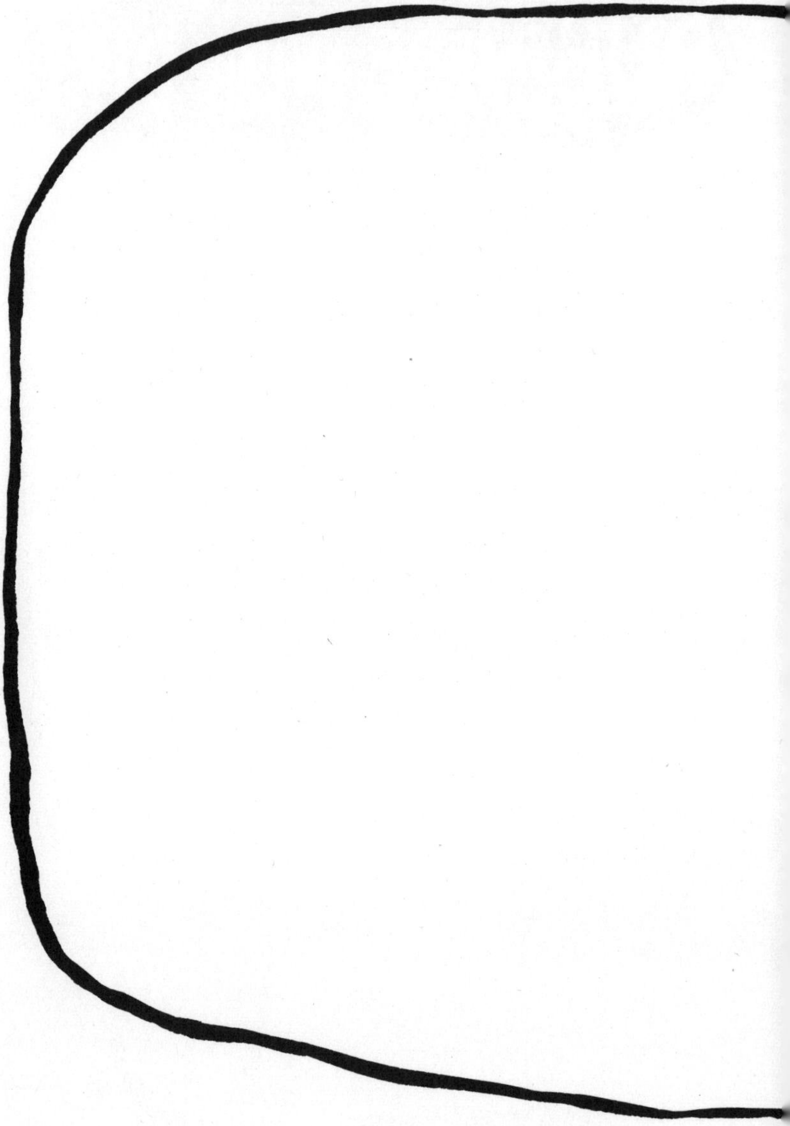

USE THIS AS A

test Page

FOR PENS, PAINTS,
MARKERS, OR ART SUPPLIES.

DRIP SOMETHING HERE.

(INK, PAINT, TEA)
CLOSE THE BOOK TO MAKE A PRINT.

Sew this page

glue A RANDOM PAGE FROM A NEWSPAPER HERE.

A PLACE FOR YOUR GROCERY LISTS.

COLLECT THE STAMPS OFF
OF ALL YOUR MAIL.

TRACE THE THINGS IN YOUR BAG (OR POCKETS). LET THE LINES OVERLAP.

COVER THIS PAGE

WITH WHITE THINGS.

scribble wildly using only borrowed pens.

(document where they were borrowed from.)

MAKE A SUDDEN, DESTRUCTIVE, UNPREDICTABLE MOVEMENT WITH THE JOURNAL.

MAKE A MESS,
CLEAN IT UP.

DOODLE OVER TOP OF:

- ☐ THE COVER.
- ☐ THE TITLE PAGE.
- ☐ THE INSTRUCTIONS.
- ☐ THE COPYRIGHT PAGE.

FOLD DOWN THE CORNERS OF YOUR FAVORITE PAGES.

Page of good thoughts.

MAKE PRINTS USING AN INK PAD AND CUT VEGETABLES.

ASK A FRIEND TO DO SOMETHING **DESTRUCTIVE** TO THIS PAGE. DON'T LOOK.

WRITE
CARELESSLY.
NOW.

GLUE RANDOM ITEMS HERE.

(i.e., things you find in your couch, on the street, etc.)

tear this page out.

PUT IT IN YOUR POCKET.
PUT IT THROUGH THE WASH.
STICK IT BACK IN.

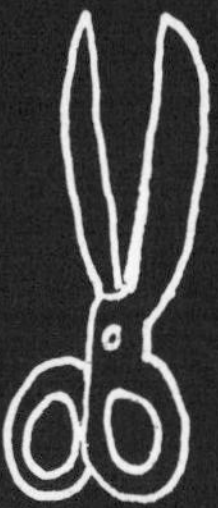

CUT
THROUGH
SEVERAL
LAYERS

Infuse this page with a smell of your choosing.

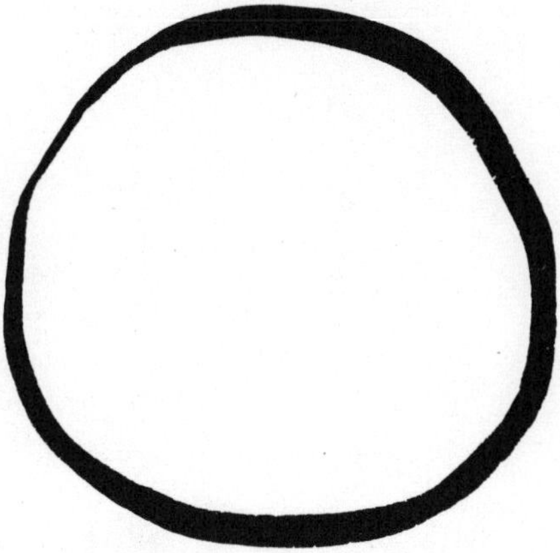

COLOR OUTSIDE OF THE LINES.

CLOSE YOUR EYES.

CONNECT THE DOTS FROM MEMORY.

HANG THE JOURNAL IN A PUBLIC PLACE.
INVITE PEOPLE TO DRAW HERE.

COLLECT YOUR

GLUE IT HERE.

↓ ↓ ↓ ↓

POCKET LINT.

trace YOUR hand.

draw with GLUE.

SAMPLE VARIOUS SUBSTANCES FOUND IN YOUR HOME.

DOCUMENT WHAT THEY ARE.

CREATE COLOR THEMES.

DOCUMENT A BORING

EVENT IN DETAIL.

CREATE A DRAWING USING A PIECE (OR SEVERAL PIECES) OF YOUR HAIR.

STICK PHOTO
HERE.

glue in a photo of
yourself you dislike.

DEFACE.

DRAW LINES USING WRITING UTENSILS (STICKS, SPOONS, TWIST TIES.

ABNORMAL

DIPPED IN INK OR PAINT.

COMB, ETC.)

fill in this page when you are really ANGRY.

WRITE OR DRAW

WITH YOUR LEFT HAND.

FIND A WAY TO WEAR THE JOURNAL.

this page is a sign.
what do you want it to say?

START

CREATE A NONSTOP

LINE.

SPACE FOR NEGATIVE COMMENTS.*

(* WHAT IS YOUR INNER CRITIC SAYING?)

DRAW LINES WITH YOUR PEN OR PENCIL.

LICK YOUR FINGER AND SMEAR THE LINES.

LOSE THIS PAGE.

(THROW IT OUT.)
ACCEPT THE LOSS.

A PAGE for FOUR-LETTER WORDS.

GLUE IN A PAGE FROM A MAGAZINE.

CIRCLE WORDS YOU LIKE.

write with the pen in your mouth.

GIVE
AWAY YOUR
FAVORITE
PAGE.

.drawkcab etirW

DOCUMENT
TIME
PASSING.

THIS SPACE IS DEDICATED

TO INTERNAL MONOLOGUE.

SCRUB THIS PAGE.

HIDE A SECRET MESSAGE SOMEWHERE IN THIS BOOK.

SLEEP WITH THE JOURNAL.

(Describe the experience here.)

CLOSE THE JOURNAL.
WRITE/SCRIBBLE SOMETHING ON THE EDGES.

WRITE A LIST OF MORE WAYS TO WRECK THIS JOURNAL.

1.

2.

3.

4.

5.

6.

7.

8.

9.

10.

11.

12.

STAIN LOG

DOODLE OVER TOP OF THIS PAGE ↓↓↓ AND IN THE MARGINS.

This is not an important piece of writing. The author of this work is writing with the intention of creating a body of text that has little or no meaning. It is merely a texture of sorts that the reader will view as a canvas. Hopefully it will simulate a book that is embedded in your memory, a book you had in your childhood, the one that you secretly wrote in with your crayons. Maybe you were scolded for this by someone.

It could be your first textbook, which you defaced with your pen, prompted by the previous owner's little scrawlings. It was not your fault. Textbooks are destined to be defaced, it is a part of their nature. You are not to be blamed. Anything as boring as a textbook deserves everything it gets.

Are you reading this? You are supposed to be defacing this page. Please stop reading at once! This is your chance to deface something.

Maybe it is not as alluring because you are being told to do it. In that case I command you to cease your drawing immediately! If you make one more mark on this page the author will personally ban you from reading any future books of hers, in perpetuity (or for as long as she continues to make books, which will probably be for a very long time).

There are many things that you could do in place of defacing this page that would be more beneficial. Some examples include going to the dentist, cleaning out your fridge, washing the windows, cleaning under your bed, reading the entire works of Proust, arranging your food alphabetically, conducting a scientific study of polymer synthesis and its effects on the world, arranging your envelopes according to size, counting how many sheets of paper you have in your possession, making sure that all of your socks have partners, documenting your pocket lint (oh, yes you already did that earlier in this book), calling your mother back, learning to speak a new language, recording yourself sleeping, moving your furniture around to simulate a bus station, experimenting with new methods of sitting that you've never tried before, jogging on the spot for an hour, pretending you are a secret agent, decorating the inside of your fridge, drawing a fake door on your wall with chalk, conversing with your animal neighbors, writing a speech for a future award, walking to the corner store as slowly as possible, writing a positive feedback letter to your mail delivery person, putting a secret note into a library book, practicing finger strengthening exercises, dressing up as your favorite author, smelling the inside of your nose, memorizing *The Elements of Style* by Strunk and White, sitting on your front porch with a sign that says "Honk if you love birds," documenting the plants in your life on paper, smelling this book, sleeping, pretending to be a famous astronaut.

FIGURE OUT A WAY
TO ATTACH THESE
TWO PAGES TOGETHER.

RUB THIS PAGE ON A DIRTY CAR.

COLLECT THE LETTER "W" HERE.

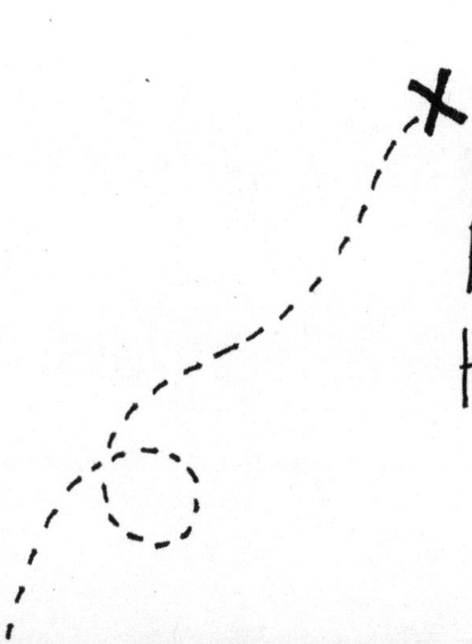

COLLECT
DEAD
BUGS
HERE.

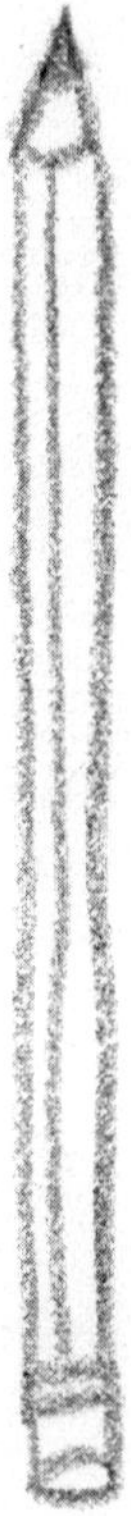

DRUM ON THIS
PAGE WITH PENCILS.

FLOAT THIS PAGE.

FIGURE OUT
A WAY TO
FREEZE
THIS PAGE.

HIDE THIS PAGE IN YOUR NEIGHBOR'S YARD.

ROLL THE JOURNAL DOWN A LARGE HILL.

SELL
THIS
PAGE.

TURN
THE
BOOK
INTO
A
SHOE.

SLIDE THE JOURNAL
(THIS PAGE FACE-DOWN),
DOWN A LONG HALLWAY.

SMUSH
SOMETHING
COLORFUL
ONTO THIS
PAGE.

SQUIRT LIQUID HERE

(TRY USING YOUR MOUTH).

COVER THIS PAGE IN TAPE

(CREATE SOME KIND OF PATTERN).

TRACE YOUR TOES.

ALSO FROM KERI SMITH

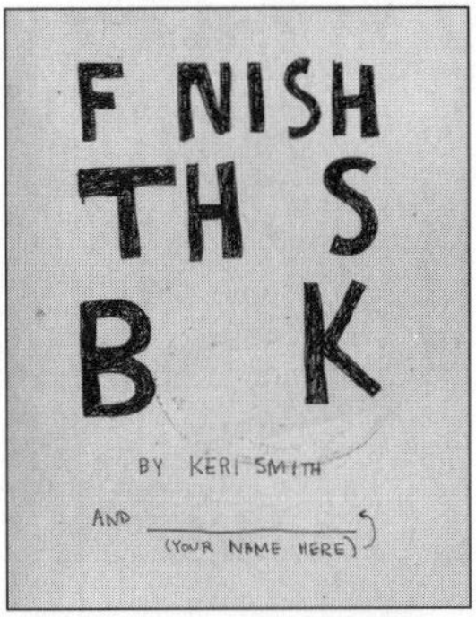

NOW AVAILABLE FOR APPLE, ANDROID, AND NOOK DEVICES!

FOR MORE INFORMATION, VISIT
PENGUIN.COM/KERISMITH • PENGUIN.COM/WRECKTHISAPP

T174.0212

THIS IS NOT A BOOK

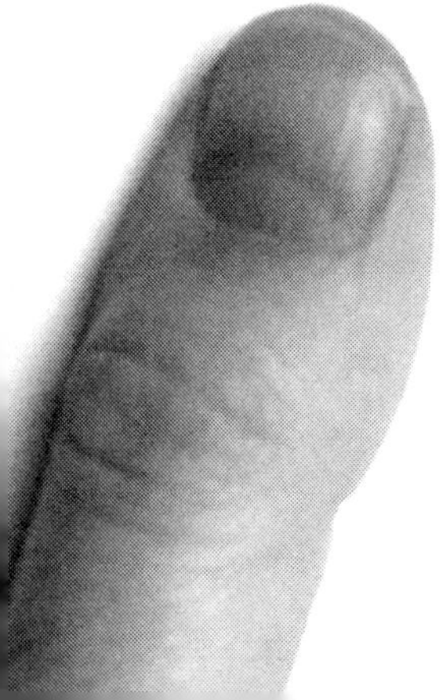

KERI SMITH

PENGUIN BOOKS

PENGUIN BOOKS
Published by the Penguin Group
Penguin Books Ltd., 80 Strand, London WC2R ORL, England
Penguin Group (USA) Inc.
375 Hudson Street, New York, New York 10014, USA
Penguin Group (Canada), 90 Eglinton Avenue East, Suite 700, Toronto, Ontario, Canada (a division of Pearson Penguin Canada Inc.) • Penguin Group Ireland, 25 St. Stephen's Green, Dublin 2, Ireland (a division of Penguin Books Ltd.) Penguin Group (Australia), 250 Camberwell Road, Camberwell, Victoria 3124, Australia (a division of Pearson Australia Group Pty. Ltd.) • Penguin Books India Pvt. Ltd., 11 Community Centre, Panchsheel Park, New Delhi – 110 017, India • Penguin Group (NZ), Cnr. Airborne and Rosedale Roads, Albany, Auckland 1310, New Zealand (a division of Pearson New Zealand Ltd.) • Penguin Books (South Africa) (Pty.) Ltd., 24 Sturdee Avenue, Rosebank, Johannesburg 2196, South Africa

Penguin Books Ltd., Registered offices: 80 Strand, London WC2R ORL, England

First published in the United States of America by Penguin Group (USA) Inc., 2009

First published in Great Britain by Penguin Books 2011

Art and design by Keri Smith.

978-1-846-14444-8
9

Printed and bound in the UK by CPI William Clowes, Beccles

NOTE TO THE READER/USER

You are about to embark on a journey. You have come to this page because the object you now hold in your hands has piqued your curiosity. You may not know exactly what it is, but that is precisely the point. In order to complete it you will be asked to do a number of things. Many of these things require the use of your imagination. You are welcome to alter this journey in any way you choose. You may complete the tasks in any time frame. Try things at different speeds to see how they change, using whatever materials you have on hand. If anything happens during the course of This Is Not a Book that you do not like, you may go back and alter it or remove it completely. You may add things you think it might need. It is your work. There are some things you need to remember:

1. TRUST IN YOUR IMAGINATION. IT IS THE SOURCE OF ALL TRUE JOURNEYS.

2. THINGS ARE NOT ALWAYS WHAT THEY SEEM.

3. ANYTHING CAN HAPPEN.

THIS IS AN INCONVENIENCE.

TAKE THIS IS NOT A BOOK EVERYWHERE YOU GO FOR ONE WEEK. YOU MUST PLACE IT IN FULL VIEW AT ALL TIMES.

THIS IS A RECORDIN

RECORD THE EVENTS OF YOUR DAY IN POINT FORM HERE:

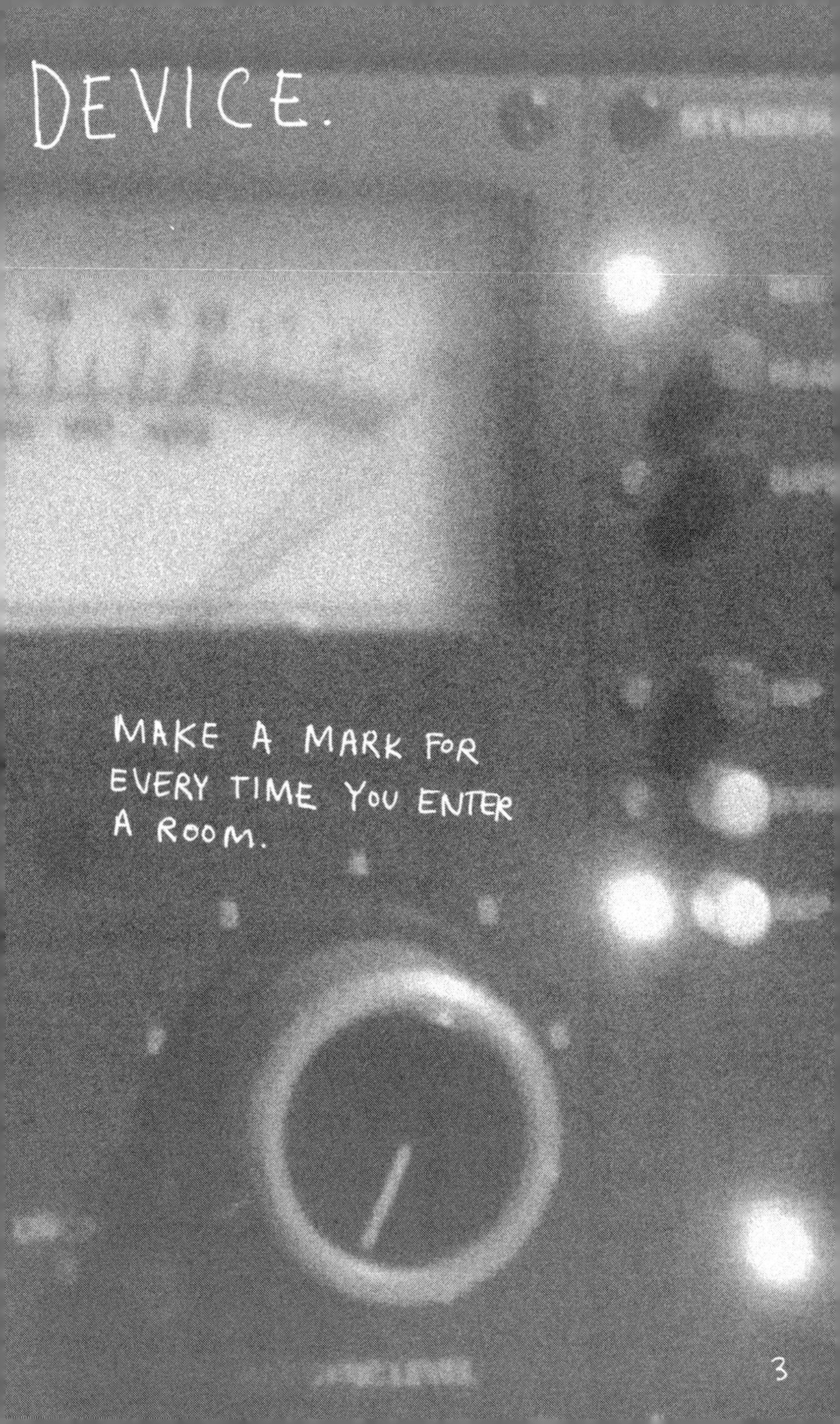
DEVICE.
MAKE A MARK FOR EVERY TIME YOU ENTER A ROOM.

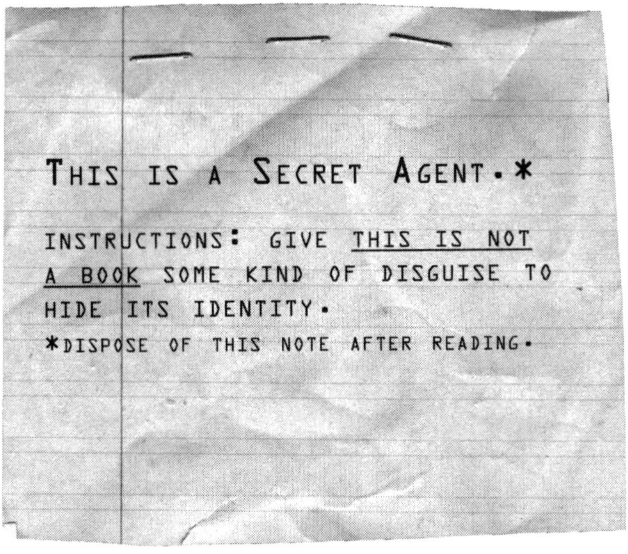

THIS IS A SECRET AGENT.*

INSTRUCTIONS: GIVE THIS IS NOT A BOOK SOME KIND OF DISGUISE TO HIDE ITS IDENTITY.

*DISPOSE OF THIS NOTE AFTER READING.

THIS IS A TEST OF ENDURANCE.

1. HOLD THIS IS NOT A BOOK ABOVE YOUR HEAD FOR AS LONG AS POSSIBLE.

2. WRITE YOUR TIME HERE: ______.

THIS IS A

NATURE EMULATOR.
AKE A BREAK ANYWHERE YOU ARE.
ADD SOME IMAGERY TO THIS SCENE.

THIS

IS

A

CHALLENGE.

PART 1:

MAKE

THIS

PAGE

AS

BIG

AS

POSSIBLE.

THIS IS A CHALLENGE.
PART 2:
MAKE THIS PAGE AS
SMALL AS POSSIBLE.

THIS IS A **THOUGHT GARDEN.**

RUMOR HAS IT, IF YOU PLANT SEEDS (IDEAS) IN THE DIRT THEY WILL GROW AND BECOME TRUE TO LIFE IN THE REAL WORLD.

PLANT YOUR IDEAS HERE.

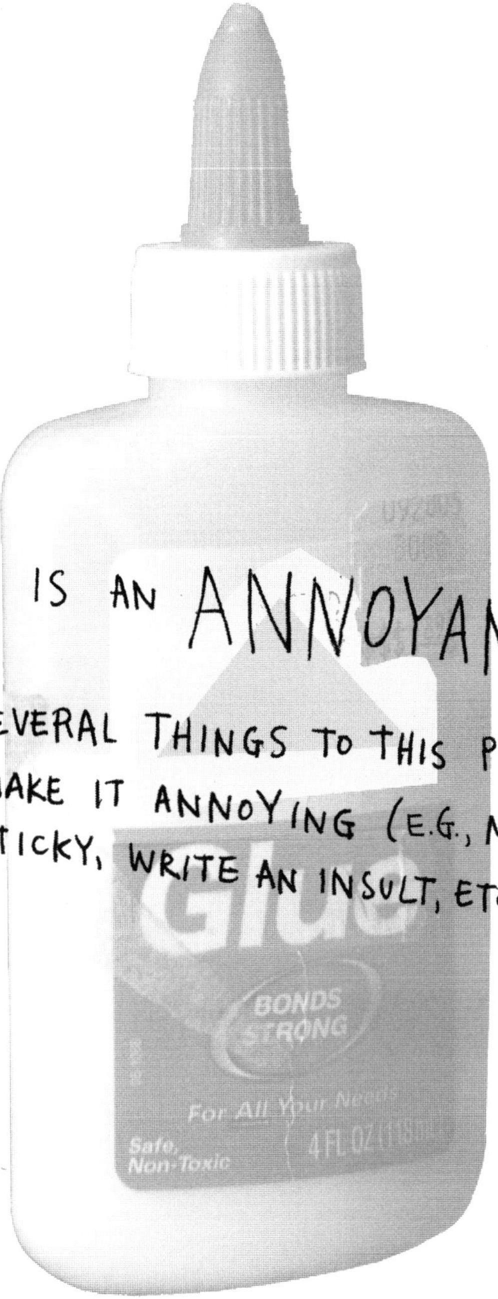

THIS IS AN ANNOYANCE.

DO SEVERAL THINGS TO THIS PAGE TO MAKE IT ANNOYING (E.G., MAKE IT STICKY, WRITE AN INSULT, ETC.).

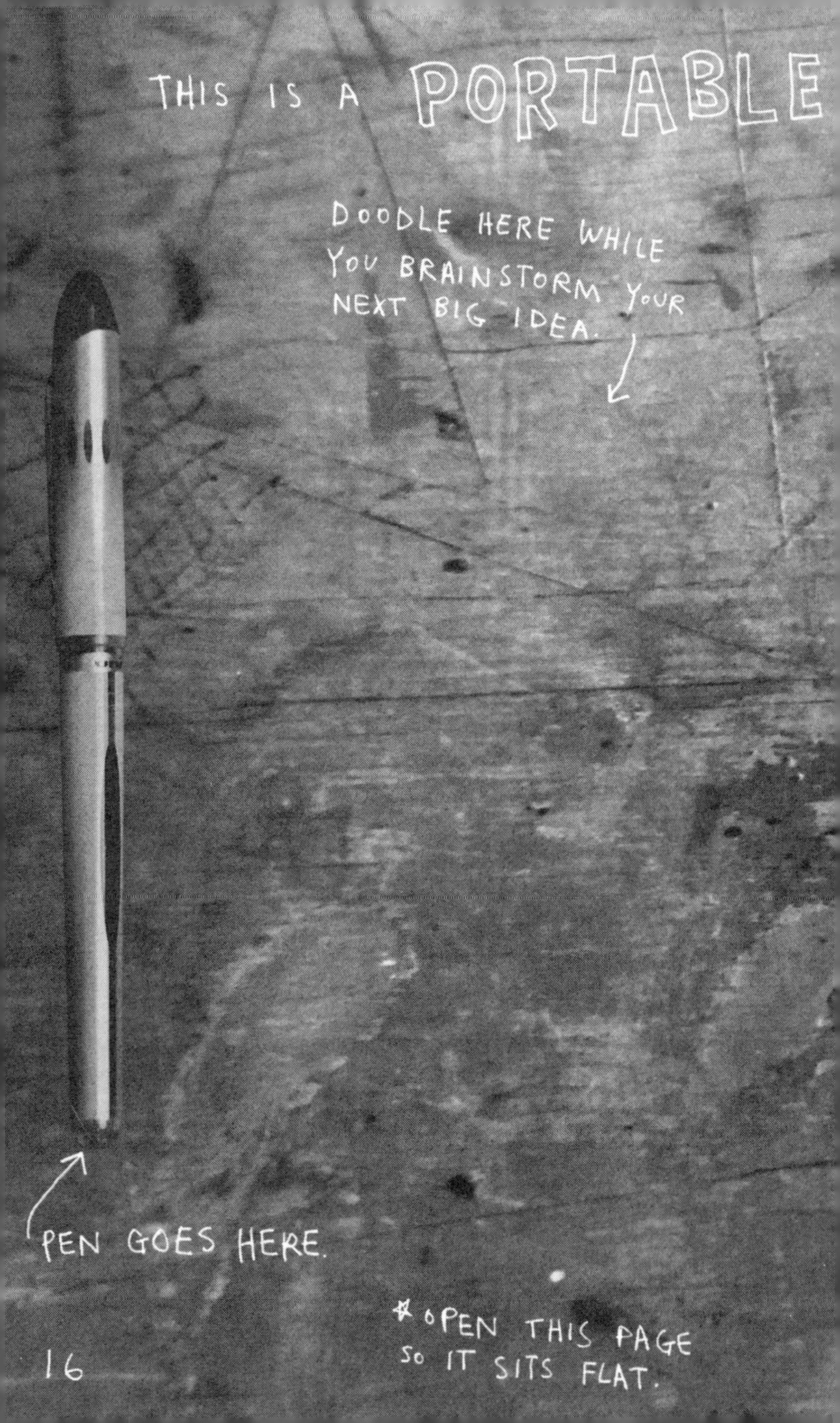

THIS IS A PORTABLE

DOODLE HERE WHILE YOU BRAINSTORM YOUR NEXT BIG IDEA.

PEN GOES HERE.

*OPEN THIS PAGE SO IT SITS FLAT.

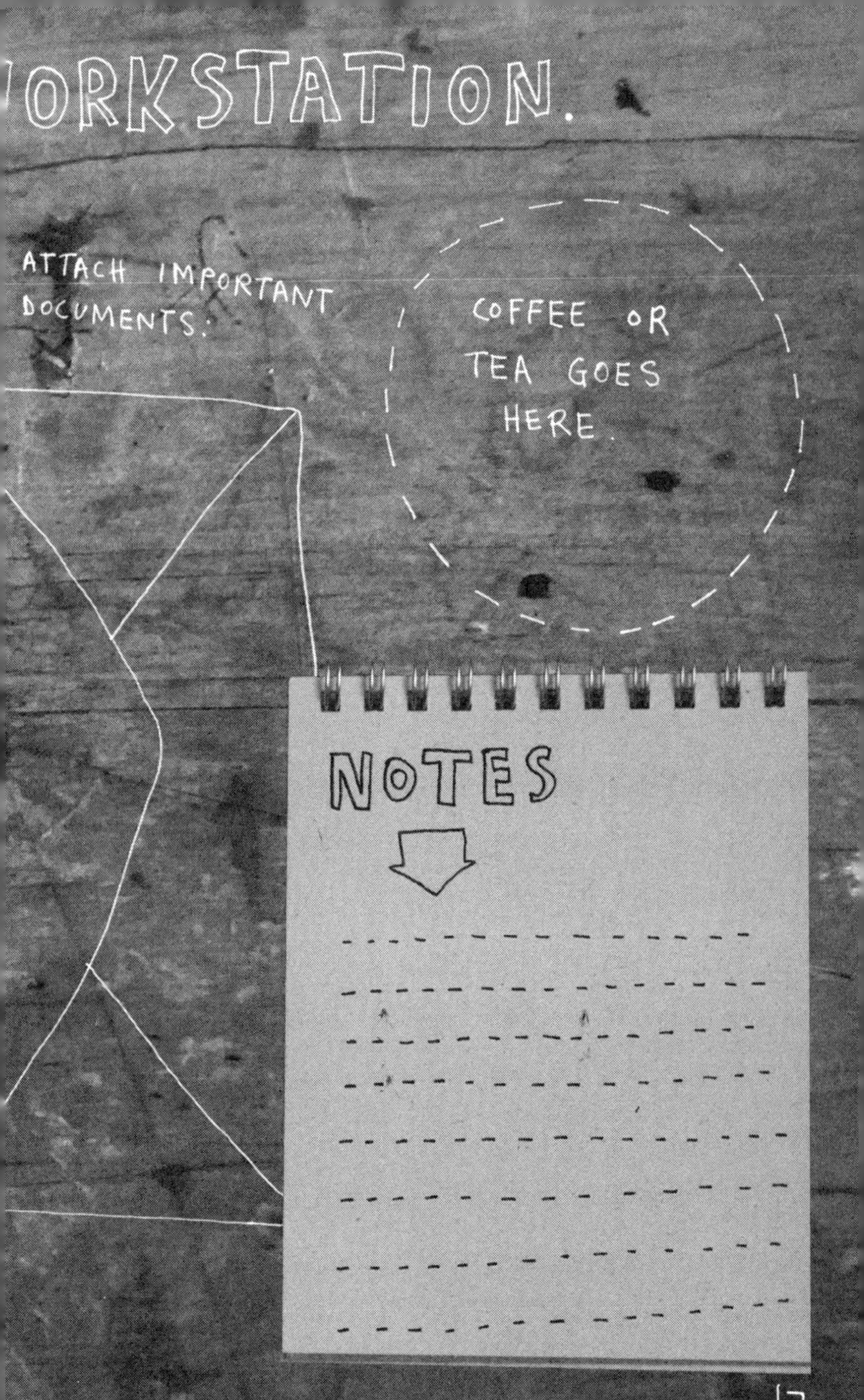
ORKSTATION.
ATTACH IMPORTANT DOCUMENTS.
COFFEE OR TEA GOES HERE.
NOTES

THIS IS A CHOICE.

1. PICK A NUMBER BETWEEN 1 AND 221.
2. GO TO THAT PAGE.
3. FLIP FORWARD FIVE PAGES. (IF YOU CANNOT, THEN FLIP BACK FIVE PAGES.)
4. DO WHATEVER IS ON THAT PAGE IMMEDIATELY.

20

THIS IS A TRANSFORMATION.

COME UP WITH A WAY TO PERMANENTLY ALTER THIS PAGE. AND CHANGE IT INTO SOMETHING COMPLETELY DIFFERENT.

THIS IS A DISAPPEARANCE.

1. DRAW OR WRITE SOMETHING HERE.
2. ERASE IT SOMEHOW (E.G., PENCIL & ERASER, WATER-SOLUBLE INK, SANDPAPER).

THIS IS A LIMITED EDITION ART PIECE.

1. EXECUTE AN IDEA ON EACH OF THESE SQUARES (IT COULD BE A DRAWING OR A THOUGHT). 2. SIGN AND DATE EACH PIECE ON THE BACK. 3. CUT THEM OUT. 4. DISPLAY THEM IN PUBLIC WITH A SIGN THAT SAYS "LIMITED EDITION ART PIECES: FREE." 5. CHECK BACK TO SEE IF ANYONE HAS TAKEN THEM.

* YOU CAN ALSO WEAR A BADGE THAT SAYS ARTIST AND STAND NEAR THE ARTWORK.

THIS IS A

BLANK SPACE.

THINK OF NOTHING.
HOW MANY EXAMPLES OF NOTHING CAN YOU THINK OF?
DRAW NOTHING HERE.

IS IS A VOYAGE.

CUT OUT PAGE.
FOLLOW FOLDING INSTRUCTIONS BELOW.
. PUT IN WATER.

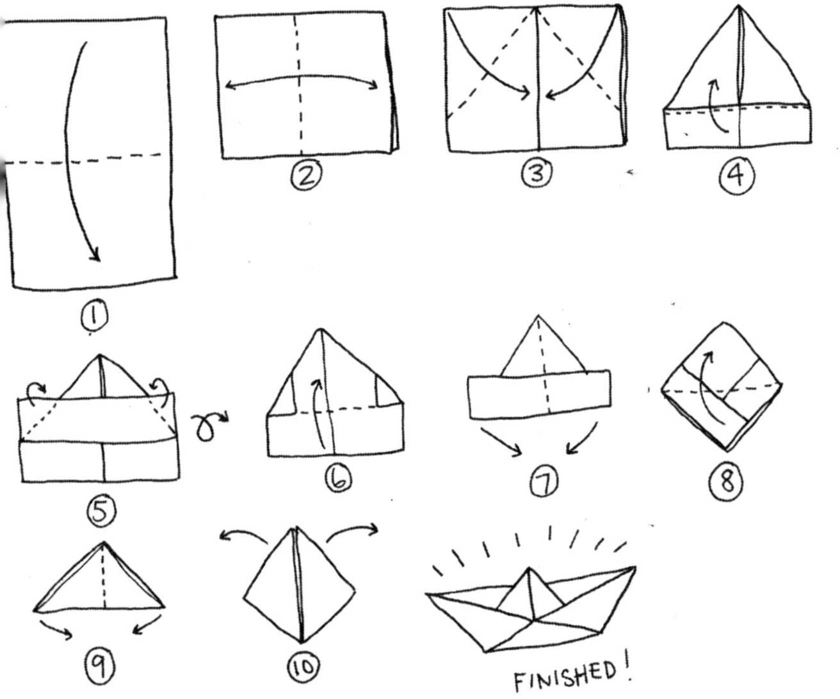

THIS IS A SECRET IDENTITY.

SECRET IDENTITY PROFILE

(WHO WOULD YOU LIKE TO BE?)

NAME:

PLACE OF BIRTH:

DATE OF BIRTH:

PROFESSION:

LIKES:

DISLIKES:

LOCATION:

LIFESTYLE SYNOPSIS (DAILY ACTIVITIES):

PERSONAL HABITS:

HOBBIES:

GROUPS & ASSOCIATIONS:

SOCIAL LIFE:

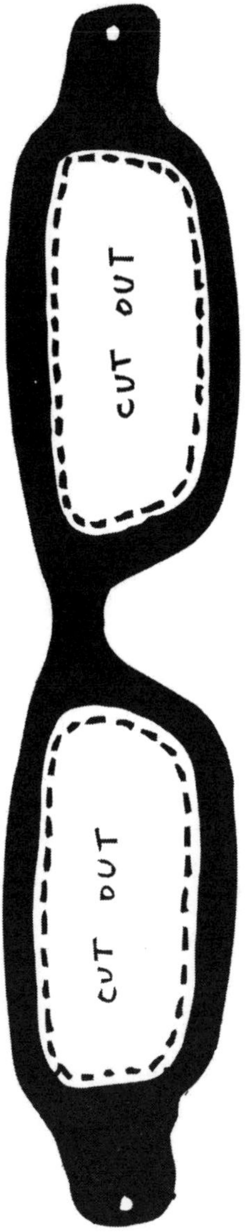
CUT OUT
CUT OUT

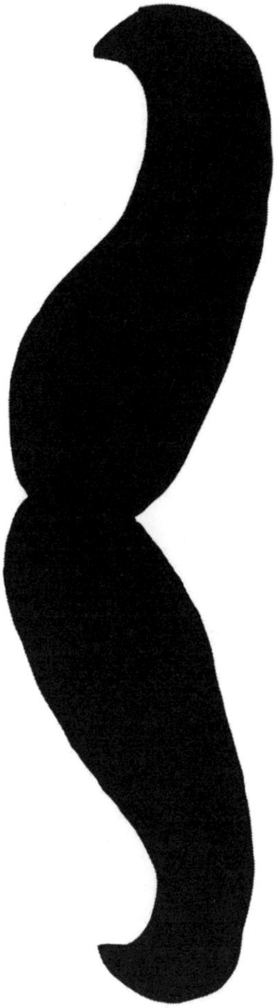

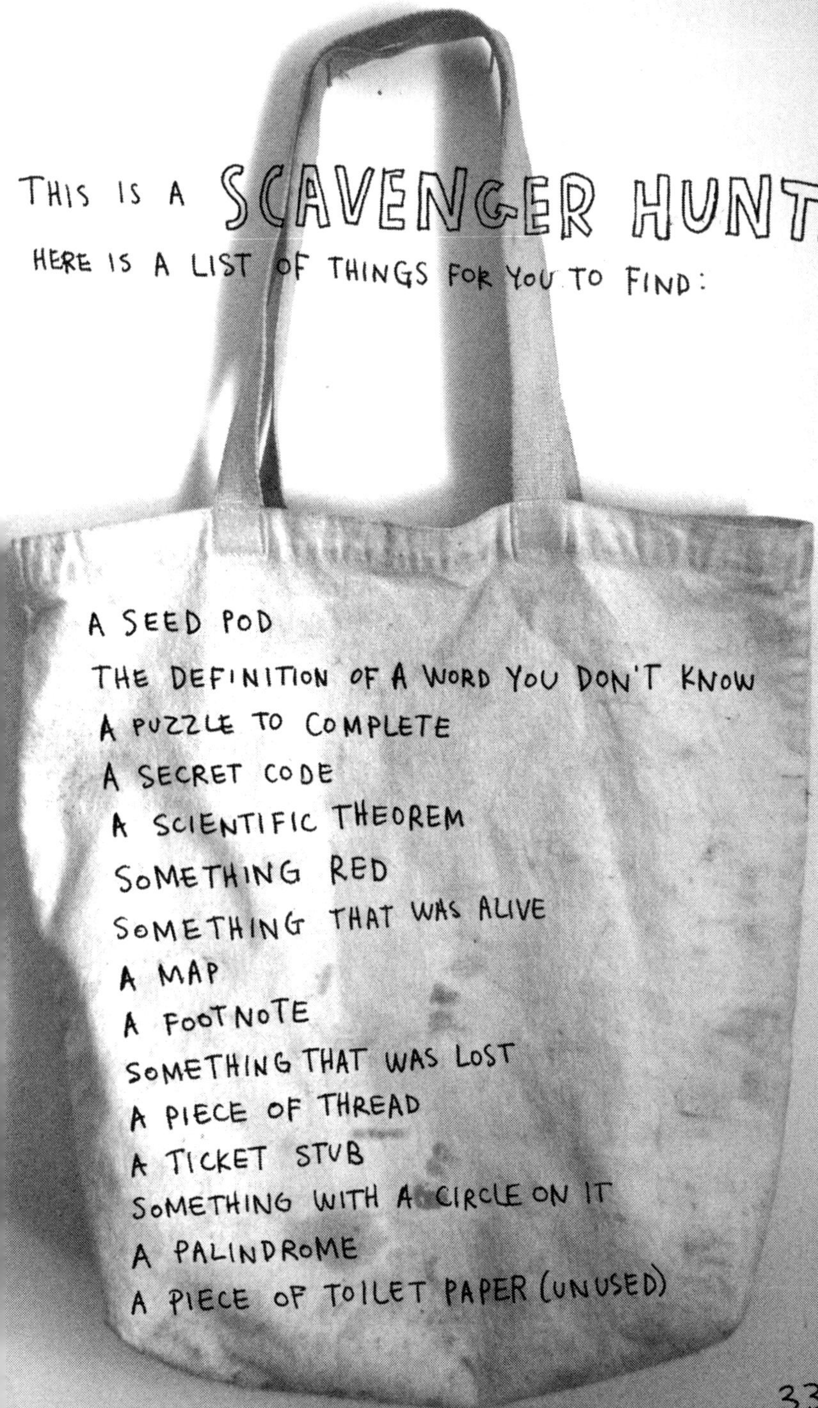

THIS IS A SCAVENGER HUNT.

HERE IS A LIST OF THINGS FOR YOU TO FIND:

A SEED POD
THE DEFINITION OF A WORD YOU DON'T KNOW
A PUZZLE TO COMPLETE
A SECRET CODE
A SCIENTIFIC THEOREM
SOMETHING RED
SOMETHING THAT WAS ALIVE
A MAP
A FOOTNOTE
SOMETHING THAT WAS LOST
A PIECE OF THREAD
A TICKET STUB
SOMETHING WITH A CIRCLE ON IT
A PALINDROME
A PIECE OF TOILET PAPER (UNUSED)

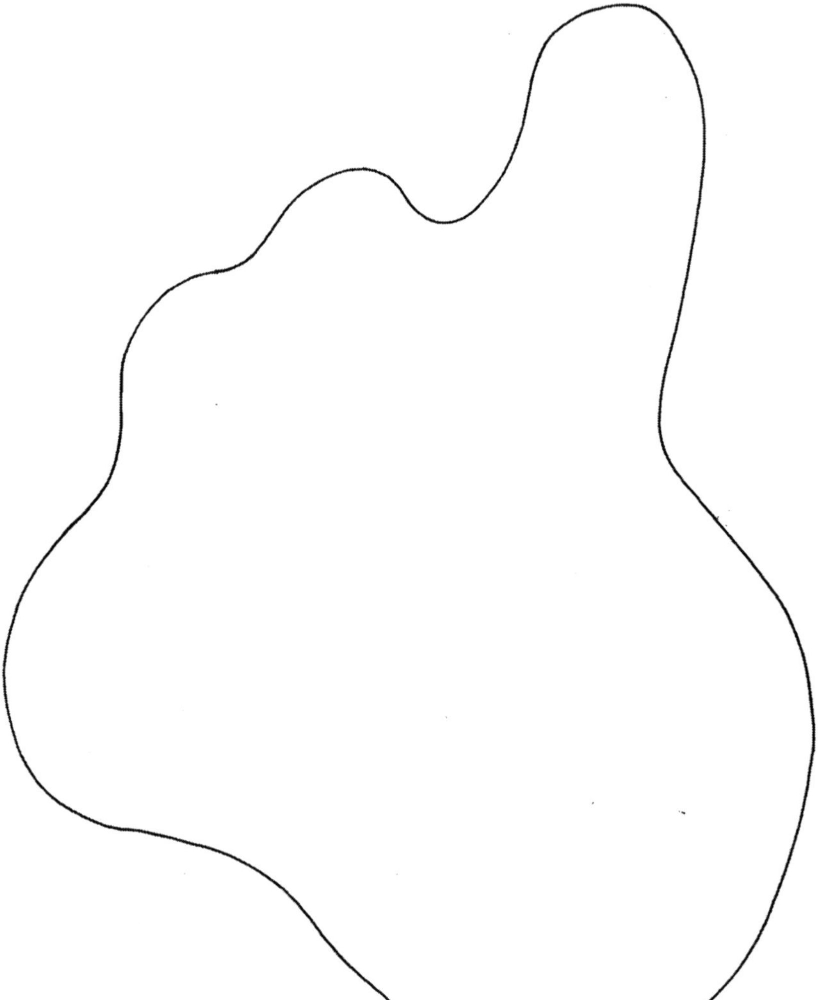

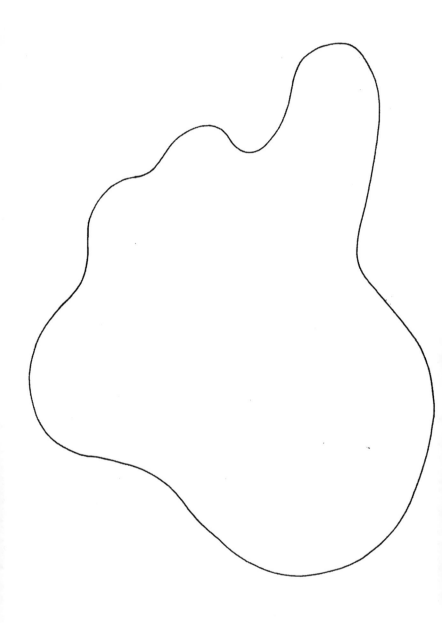

THIS IS A PLAYGROUND.

COLOR IN THIS SHAPE USING THE STRANGEST METHOD YOU CAN THINK OF (E.G., MAKE YOUR WRITING UTENSIL REALLY LONG BY ATTACHING SOMETHING TO IT WITH TAPE).

THIS IS A CHAIN LETTER.

1. CUT OUT THE LETTER.
2. UNDER "ORIGINATOR" PUT YOUR NAME & ADDRESS.
3. SEND LETTER TO ONE FRIEND.

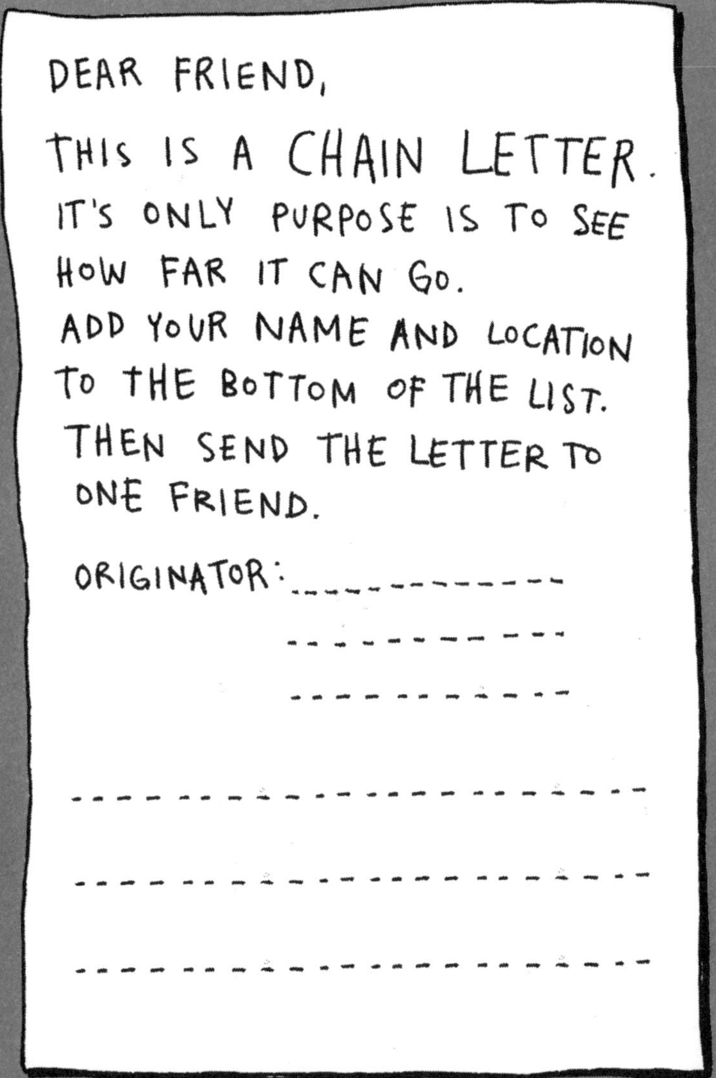
DEAR FRIEND,

THIS IS A CHAIN LETTER.
IT'S ONLY PURPOSE IS TO SEE HOW FAR IT CAN GO.
ADD YOUR NAME AND LOCATION TO THE BOTTOM OF THE LIST.
THEN SEND THE LETTER TO ONE FRIEND.

ORIGINATOR: ____________

THIS IS A COMMENT.

1. FILL IN A THOUGHT.
2. LEAVE IN A PUBLIC PLACE.

THIS IS AN ACTION SCULPTURE.

COME UP WITH AN INTERESTING WAY TO MAKE THIS IS NOT A BOOK MOVE (E.G., TIE AN UMBRELLA TO THE SPINE. DROP FROM A HEIGHT).

THIS IS A SET OF DIRECTIONS.

1. GET A WRITING UTENSIL (PEN, PENCIL, ETC.).
2. CHOOSE A STARTING POINT.
3. DRAW A STRAIGHT LINE IN ANY DIRECTION; STOP BEFORE YOU GET TO THE EDGE OF THE PAGE.
4. DRAW A CURVY LINE IN THE OPPOSITE DIRECTION.
5. ADD A SQUARE. COLOR IT IN.
6. FROM ONE OF THE CORNERS OF THE SQUARE DRAW A DOTTED LINE ON A DIAGONAL, ABOUT TWO INCHES LONG.
7. AT THE END OF THE DOTTED LINE DRAW A CIRCLE.
8. INSIDE THE CIRCLE WRITE THE NAME OF THE LAST PERSON YOU SPOKE TO.
9. FROM THE CIRCLE DRAW A LINE TO ONE OF THE CORNERS OF THE PAGE.
10. FOLD THE CORNER DOWN AND COLOR IT IN.
11. FROM THAT CORNER DRAW A VERY FAT LINE TO THE MIDDLE OF THE PAGE.
12. DRAW THE MOON HERE.
13. SIGN YOUR NAME.

THIS IS A FRIEND.

TURN THIS IS NOT A BOOK OR OTHER OBJECTS INTO CHARACTERS BY ADDING THESE ITEMS.

*PHOTO IS ACTUAL SIZE.

THIS IS A FACTORY
THAT CREATES VERY SMALL BOOKS
BY UNKNOWN AUTHORS.

THE FACTORY ITSELF IS VERY SMALL.*

1. CUT OUT TEMPLATE BELOW ALONG SOLID LINES.
2. ASSEMBLE ACCORDING TO DIAGRAM.
3. ADD CONTENT.
4. CONTINUE PRODUCTION.

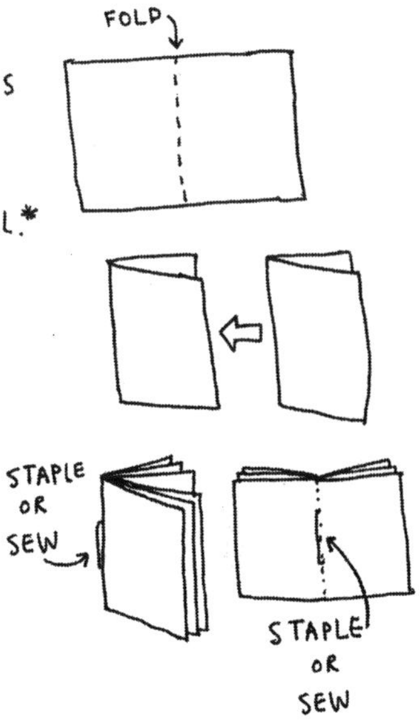

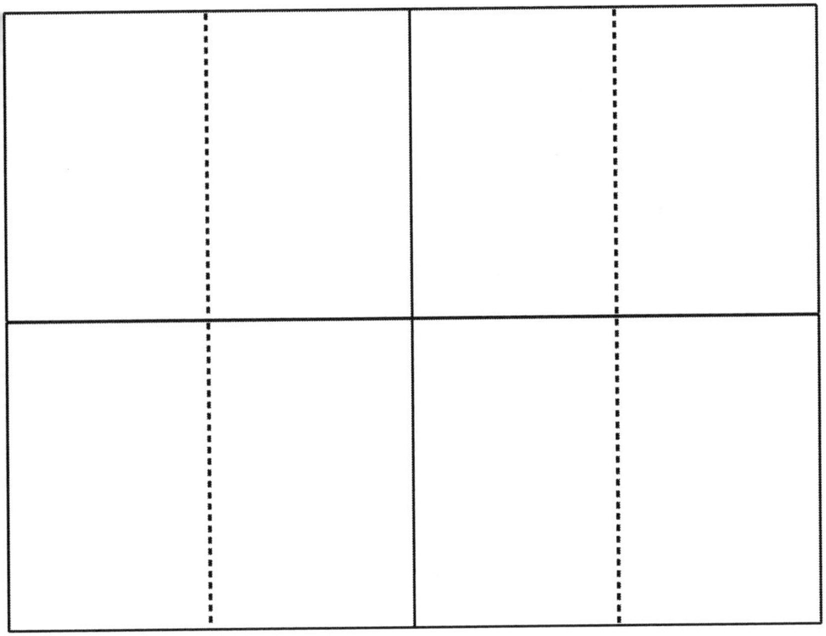

THIS IS A FORM OF *communication.*

1. WRITE A MESSAGE FOR SOMEONE HERE.
2. GIVE MESSAGE TO RECIPIENT.
3. WAIT FOR RESPONSE.
4. PASS <u>THIS IS NOT A BOOK</u> BACK AND FORTH.*

*IF THE RECIPIENT LIVES FAR AWAY, MAIL <u>THIS IS NOT A BOOK</u> BACK AND FORTH.

THIS IS A CONCEALMENT.

USE THIS PAGE TO COVER UP A PAGE THAT YOU DON'T LIKE.

THIS IS A

HIDING PLACE.

STASH YOUR SECRETS HERE.

THIS IS AN IMAGINARY *place*.

THIS IS YOUR VERY OWN PLANET.
YOU MUST ADD THINGS TO IT TO MAKE IT FLOURISH.

1. CREATE A LEGEND WITH SYMBOLS TO ADD BUILDINGS, PEOPLE, AND THINGS FROM YOUR IMAGINATION.
2. DESRIBE THE WEATHER AND THE INHABITANTS; ADD ROADS, ETC.

THIS IS A TIME TRAVEL DEVICE

1. THINK OF A TIME AND PLACE YOU WOULD LIKE TO REVISIT. ENTER IT ON THE SCREEN BELOW.

2. MAKE DETAILED NOTES INCLUDING EVERYTHING YOU CAN REMEMBER ABOUT THAT TIME—COLORS, SMELLS, LIGHT, TIME OF DAY, NAMES, SPACE.

ALTERNATE: WRITE ABOUT A FUTURE TIME AND PLACE USING YOUR IMAGINATION.

THIS IS AN

ETHNOGRAPHIC STUDY.

1. GO TO A PUBLIC PLACE.
2. PRETEND YOU ARE AN ALIEN VISITING THE PLANET FOR THE FIRST TIME.
3. TAKE NOTES ABOUT HUMAN BEHAVIOR AND HUMAN CUSTOMS AS IF YOU'VE NEVER SEEN THEM BEFORE.

[T]HIS IS A COMMITMENT.

DO ONE THING ON THIS LIST EVERY DAY FOR ONE MONTH.

WEAR AN ARTICLE OF CLOTHING INSIDE OUT
READ A BOOK YOU DON'T THINK YOU WILL LIKE
SING ON YOUR WAY TO WORK/SCHOOL
GIVE SOMETHING AWAY
TAKE A PHOTO
DRAW SOMETHING
WRITE A LETTER

63

HIS IS A RANDOM OCCURRENCE.

. DROP A STRING ONTO THIS PAGE.
. TRACE THE STRING.
. REPEAT.

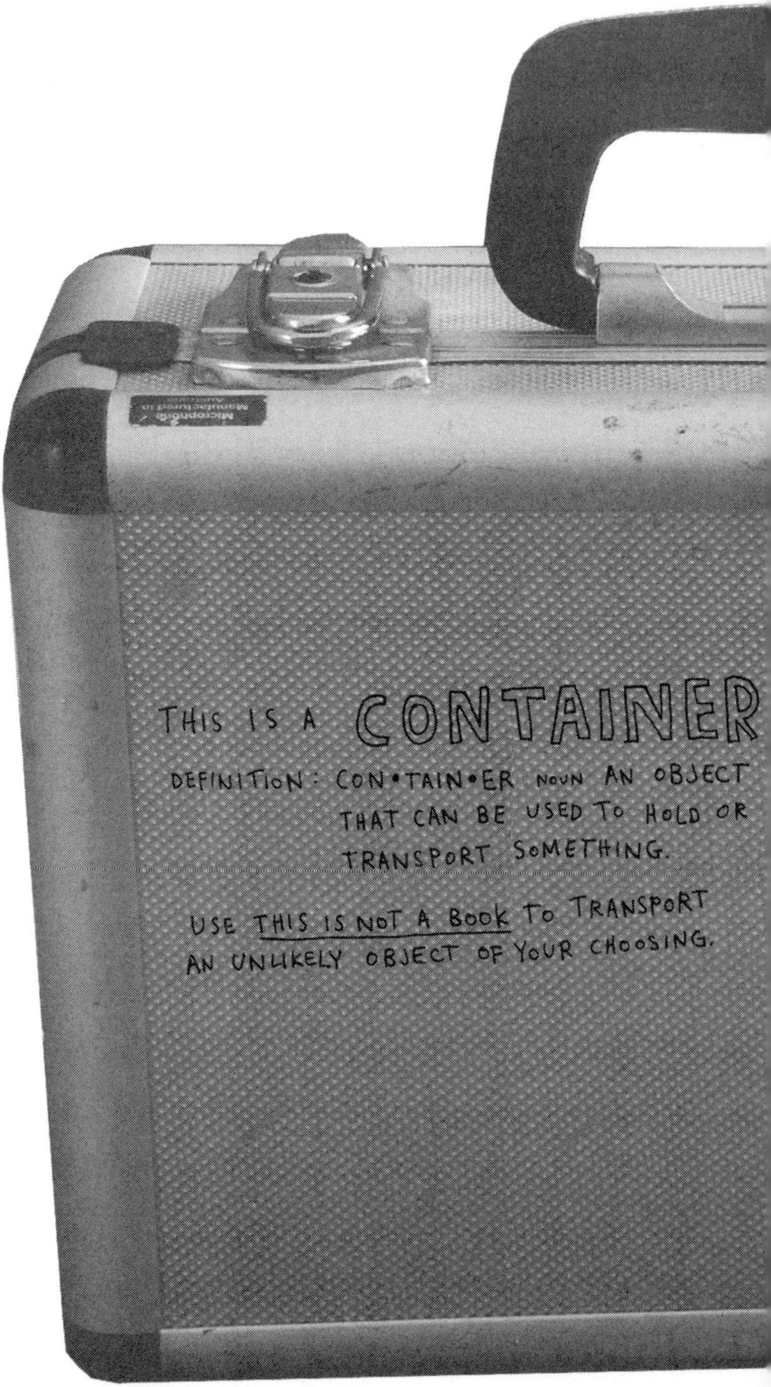

THIS IS A CONTAINER

DEFINITION: CON•TAIN•ER NOUN AN OBJECT THAT CAN BE USED TO HOLD OR TRANSPORT SOMETHING.

USE THIS IS NOT A BOOK TO TRANSPORT AN UNLIKELY OBJECT OF YOUR CHOOSING.

THIS IS A **LOST TREASURE.**

1. FIND A GOOD HIDING SPOT FOR <u>THIS IS NOT A BOOK</u>.
2. CREATE A "TREASURE MAP."
3. GIVE THE MAP TO A FRIEND AND INSTRUCT THEM TO FIND IT.

THE CENTRAL REGISTRY'S
APPLICATION FOR PAGE USAGE

TO BE COMPLETED BY APPLICANT (PLEASE PRINT*):

SECTION 1

APPLICANT'S NAME ____________________ PHONE(S) (PLEASE LIST ALL PHONE NUMBERS YOU HAVE EVER HAD)**____________________ SHOE SIZE _______

ADDRESS ____________________________ BIRTHDAY ____________________

MOTHER'S MAIDEN NAME _________ MOTHER'S MOTHER'S MOTHER'S MAIDEN NAME _______________________ FAVORITE COLOR _____________

TIME YOU WENT TO SLEEP LAST FRIDAY NIGHT _____ DOMINANT HAND L R

CIRCLE DAY OF THE WEEK M T W TH F S S

SECTION 2

PLEASE STATE THE REASON YOU ARE APPLYING FOR USAGE OF THIS PAGE.

____

PLEASE DESCRIBE WHAT YOU HAD FOR BREAKFAST THIS MORNING.

____

PLEASE WRITE YOUR BEST FRIEND'S NAME WHILE TOUCHING YOUR NOSE.

____

STATE THE LAST TIME YOU FILLED OUT A FORM. FOR WHAT PURPOSE?

____

SECTION 3

DRAW AN OFFICIAL STAMP HERE.

INSTRUCTIONS**

1. STAPLE A PHOTO OF YOURSELF TO THIS FORM.
2. CUT OUT SECTION 3 AND ATTACH IT TO PAGE 32 OF THIS IS NOT A BOOK.
3. SIGN AND DATE THIS FORM.
4. PLEASE FILL OUT THIS FORM IN TRIPLICATE.
5. IN ORDER TO PROCESS THIS FORM YOU MUST HAVE THE BLESSING OF A NEIGHBO

*INCCORRECT SPELLING WILL VOID APPLICATION.

**IF ANSWERS DO NOT FIT IN SPACE ALLOTTED, PLEASE ATTACH AN ADDITIONAL FORM.

OFFICE COPY FORM **#253HD459208**

THIS IS A BUREAUCRACY.

1. FILL OUT THIS FORM.

2. FOLLOW INSTRUCTIONS AT BOTTOM OF FORM.

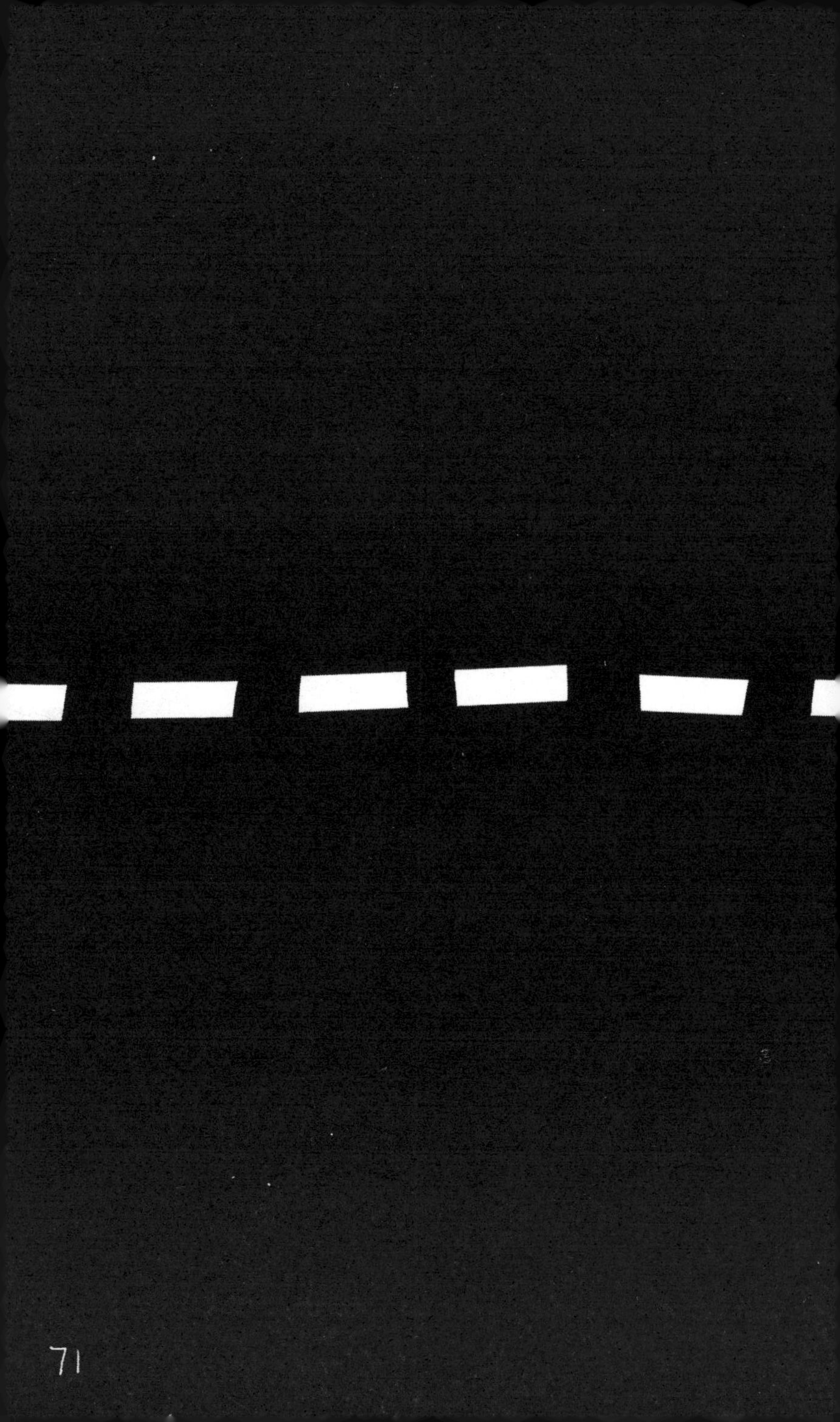

THIS IS A BORDER.

PLACE THIS IN A LOCATION IN WHICH YOU WOULD LIKE TO MAKE A SEPARATION BETWEEN TWO AREAS. YOU MAY WISH TO WRITE A NOTE ON EACH SIDE EXPLAINING WHAT THE SPACE IS DESIGNATED FOR (E.G., PUBLIC VS. PRIVATE, MINE VS. YOURS).

THIS IS AN EMBELLISHMENT.

USE THIS FRAME TO EMBELLISH ANOTHER PAGE.

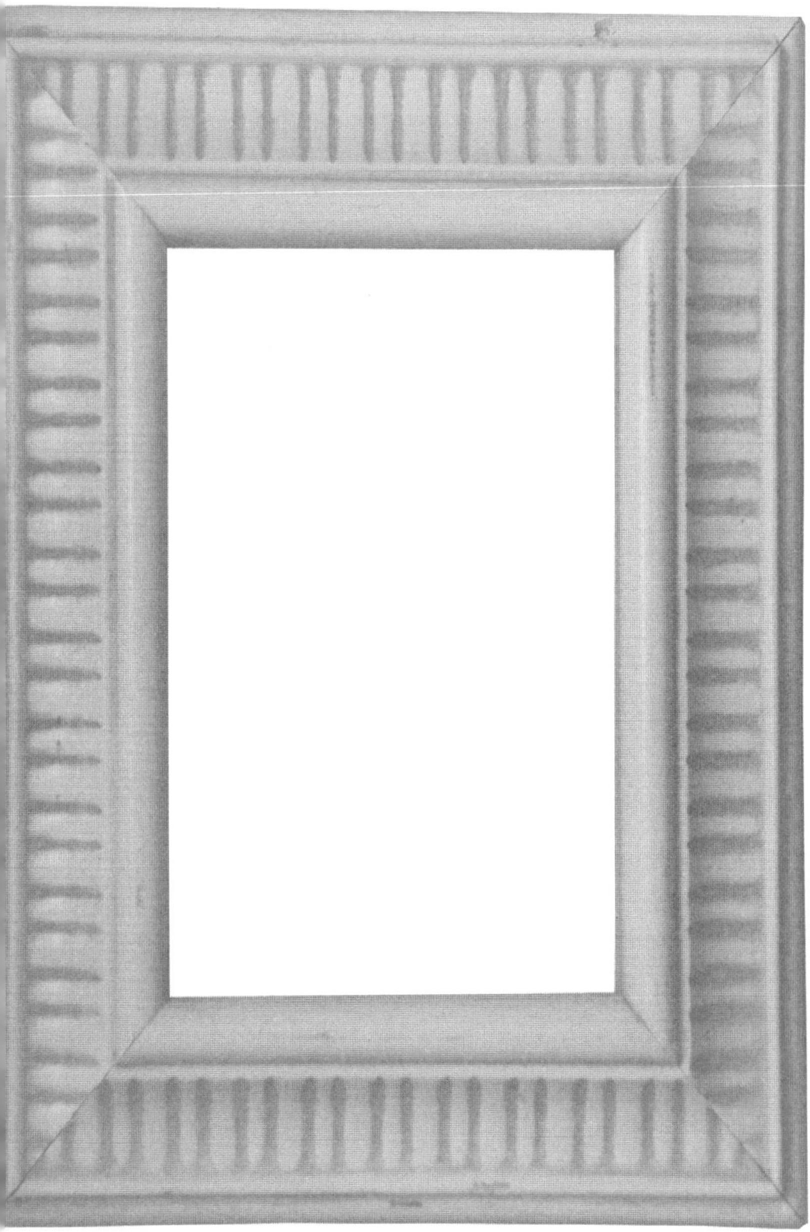

THIS IS A

RESEARCH PROJECT

1. FIND AN ENCYCLOPEDIA.
2. OPEN IT UP TO A RANDOM PAGE.
3. CLOSE YOUR EYES AND POINT.
4. WRITE DOWN THE SUBJECT YOU HAVE CHOSEN.
5. FIND OUT MORE ABOUT THIS SUBJECT. WRITE DOWN ANY FACTS YOU FIND. BECOME AN EXPERT.

THIS IS AN
ESCAPE CAPSULE.
THE SIZE OF THE CAPSULE IS QUITE LIMITED (THE SIZE OF A SMALL CLOSET).
1. MAKE A LIST OF THINGS YOU WOULD PUT IN YOUR CASULE.
2. DECORATE THIS PAGE WITH PHOTOS, WRITINGS, AND IMAGERY THAT YOU REALLY ENJOY (TO ACCOMPANY YOU IN THE CAPSULE).

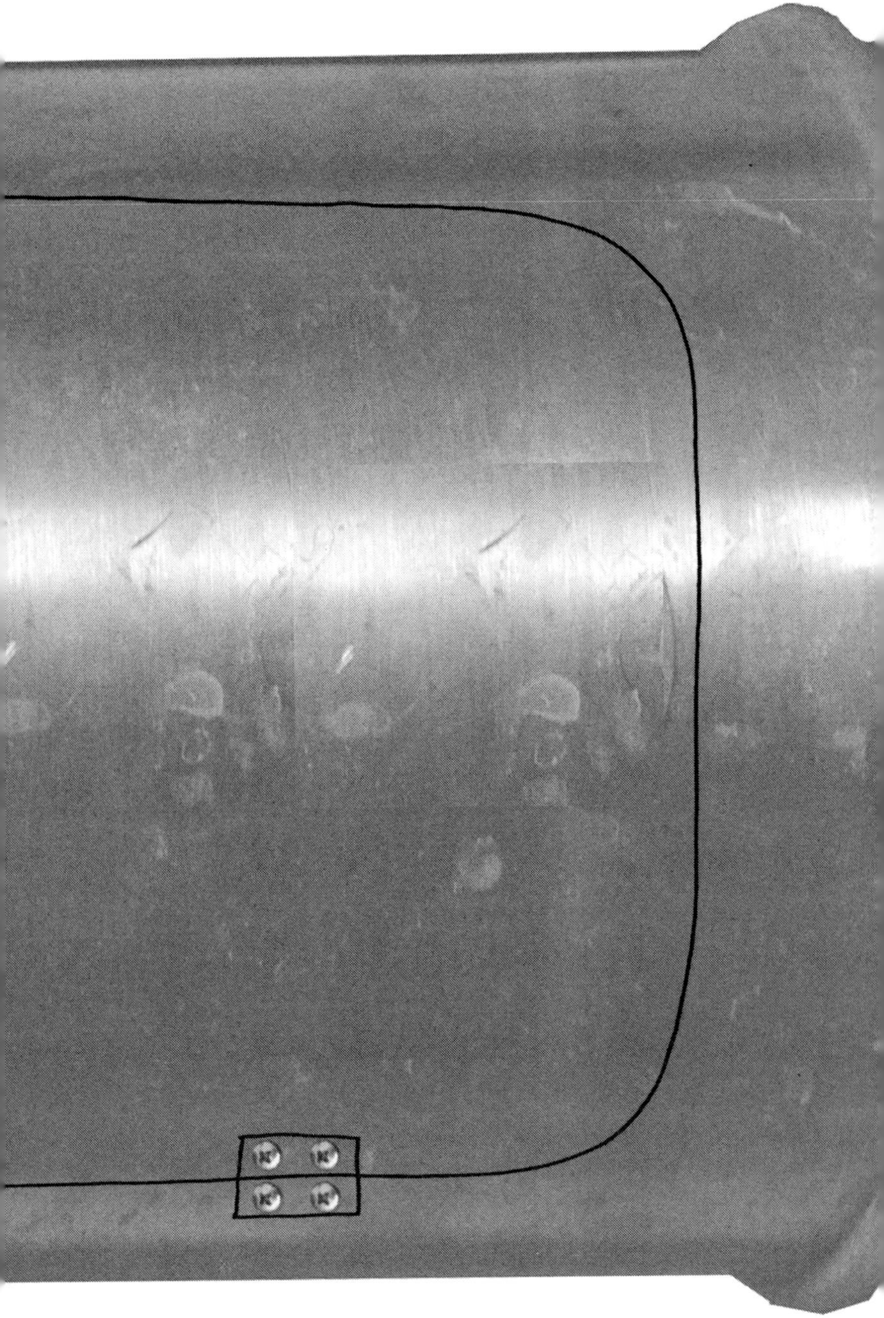

THIS IS A GROUP ACTIVITY.

1. ASSEMBLE A GROUP OF PEOPLE.
2. WHILE STANDING, HAVE A CONTEST TO SEE WHO CAN BALANCE _THIS IS NOT A BOOK_ ON SOME PART OF THEIR BODY (EXCLUDING THE HEAD) FOR THE LONGEST PERIOD OF TIME.

ALTERNATE: WHILE WALKING, PLACE THIS IS NOT A BOOK BETWEEN YOUR LEGS. SEE WHO CAN WALK THE FARTHEST.

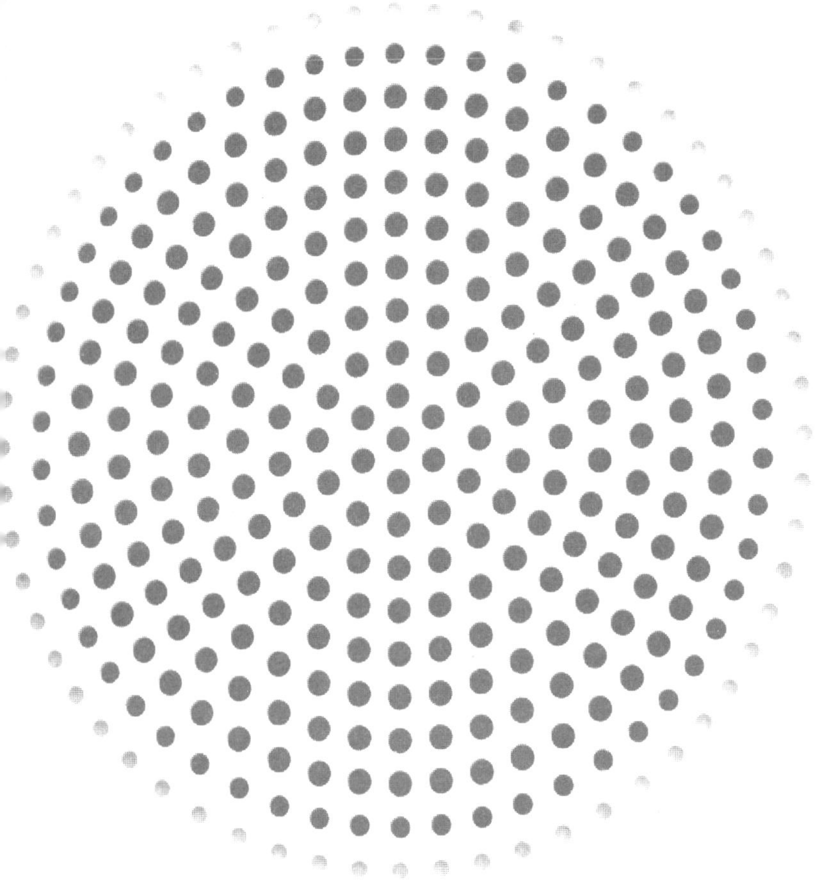

THIS IS A *guest registry.**
* FOR FRIENDS OR VISITORS
YOUR COMMENTS ARE MOST WELCOME.

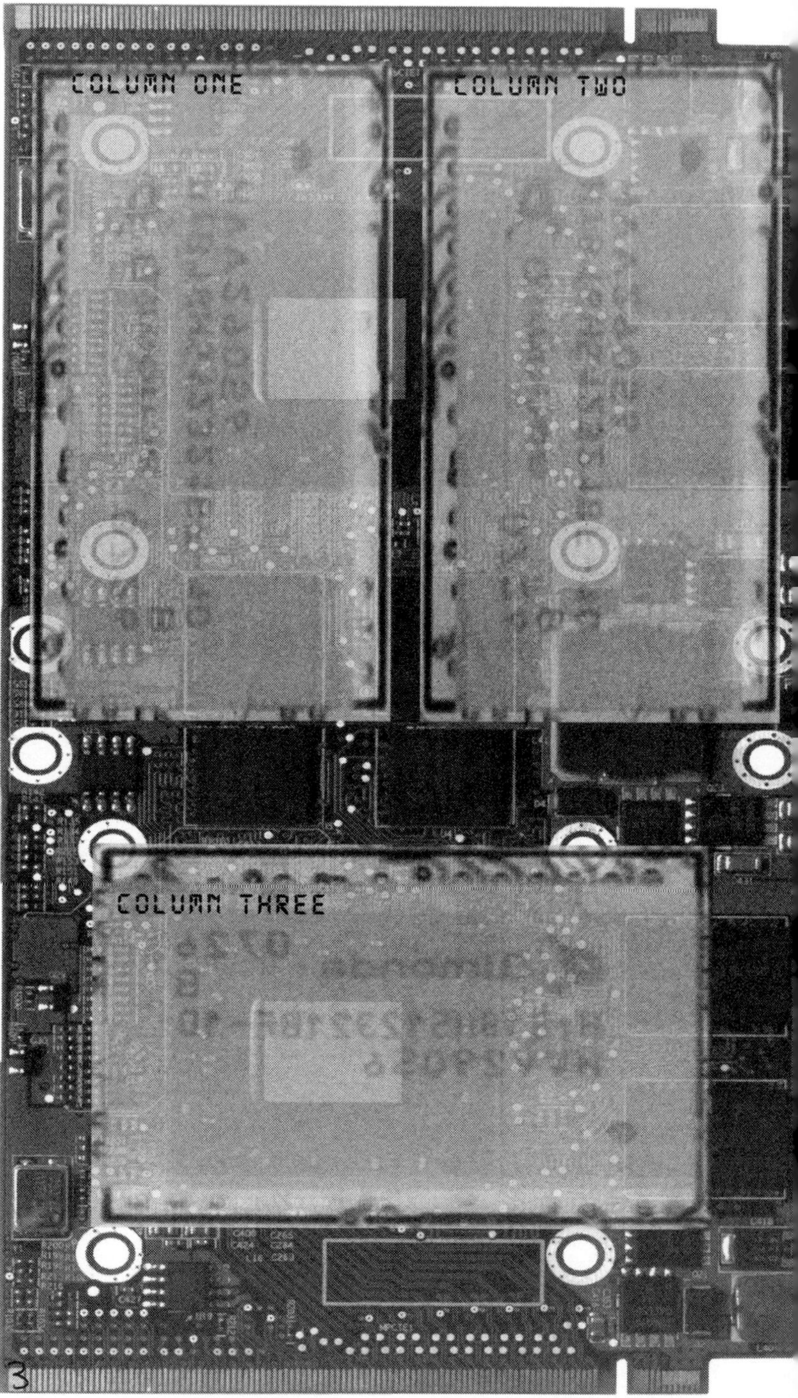
COLUMN ONE
COLUMN TWO
COLUMN THREE

THIS IS AN

IDEA FORMULATION GENERATOR.

1. IN COLUMN ONE MAKE A LIST OF THINGS FOUND IN NATURE.
2. IN COLUMN TWO MAKE A LIST OF OBJECTS YOU USE EVERY DAY.
3. IN COLUMN THREE MAKE A LIST OF WORDS YOU LIKE.
4. PICK ONE ITEM FROM EACH LIST AND COMBINE THEM TO COME UP WITH AN IDEA FOR A NEW PRODUCT OR CONCEPT.

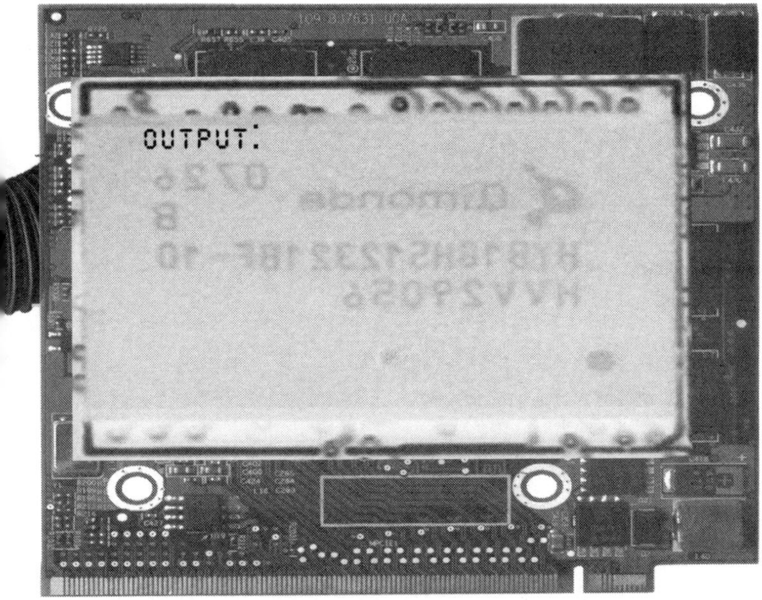

THIS IS A GROUPING OF CIRCLES WITH NO PURPOSE WHATSOEVER.

DRAW THEM USING WHATEVER METHODS YOU PREFER.

THIS A **METHODOLOGY**

FOR INVESTIGATING THE PRACTICE OF CARRYING THINGS THAT ARE NOT BOOKS.

1. TEST EACH OF THESE METHODS.
2. COME UP WITH FIVE MORE.

THIS IS A HABITAT.

FOR MICROORGANISMS. PLEASE HELP THEM TO FEEL AT HOME BY ADDING A VARIETY OF THINGS (FURNITURE, ROOMS, HOUSES, WALKWAYS, ETC.). MAKE THEM AS SMALL AS POSSIBLE.

THIS IS A TELEVISION.

YOU GET TO DO ALL YOUR OWN PROGRAMMING.

1. WRITE YOUR OWN SHOW.
2. MAKE A THREE-DIMENSIONAL DIORAMA OF YOUR SHOW OUT OF CARDBOARD.
3. USE THE TV AS A FRAME.

CUT
OUT

93

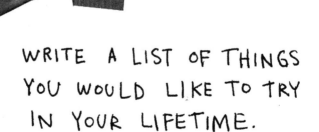

WRITE A LIST OF THINGS
YOU WOULD LIKE TO TRY
IN YOUR LIFETIME.

THIS IS A

WISHING WELL.

1. WRITE A WISH.
2. TAPE MONEY HERE.

AAAAAAVVVVVVMMMMMMTTTTTT
WWWWMMMMRRRRRRGGGGGG
IIIIIOOOOOOOLLLLLLWWWWW
QQQQQQNNNNNNCCCCCCSSSSSS
DDDDDDEEEEEEEEFFFFFJJJJJJ
SSSSTHISISAHIDDENMESSAGEOO
HHHHHEEEEEEEEWWWWWPPPP
AAAAAABBBBBBBBKKKKKKFFFFF
NNNNFINDAWAYTOHIDEAMESSA
GESOMEWHEREINTHISISNOTABO
OKSOTHATNOONECANFINDITAAA
TTTTTUUUUUUUPPPPPPPHHHH
SSSSSSGOODLUCKAAAAANNNNN
KKKKKKKKKEEEEEEEEAAAAAAA
NNNNNNNSSSSSSSWWWWWEEEE
YYYYYYYIIIIIIIOOOOOOXXXXXX
RRRRRRREEEEEEEEAAAAADDDD
MMMMOOOOOOOOOORRRREEEE
BBBBBBBOOOOOOOOOOOKKKKK
SSSSSSSSSEEEEEEEEAAAATTTTT
YYYYYYYOOOOOOOOUUUUUURRR
GGGGGGGGGRRRRRREEEEEEEEE
NNNNNNSSSSSSYYYYYOOOOUUU
AAAARRRRRRREEEEEEEEGGGGGG
RRRRRREEEEEEEEAAAAAATTTTTTT

THIS IS AN EXPERIMENT.
LEAVE THIS IS NOT A BOOK
SOMEWHERE OVERNIGHT.

100

THIS IS A MAP.

CREATE A MAP BASED ON SOME ASPECT OF YOUR EVERYDAY LIFE. SOME EXAMPLES MIGHT BE YOUR DESK, YOUR WALK TO SCHOOL OR WORK, YOUR DINNER TABLE, YOUR HAND.

THIS IS A PSYCHOLOGICAL MOOD-ALTERING MACHINE.

1. WRITE ABOUT YOUR CURRENT MOOD IN DETAIL IN THE SPACE PROVIDED.
2. ENTER YOUR MOOD OF CHOICE ON THE MACHINE BELO
3. FOCUS REALLY HARD ON WHAT YOUR MOOD OF CHOICE FEELS LIKE.
4. ALLOW FOR MOOD TRANSITION TO TAKE PLACE. (MAY TAKE A FEW HOURS

CAUTION: UNIT MUST BE WIRED
CORRECTLY. SEE OWNERS GUIDE.
CLASS 2 WIRING MAY BE USED © CROWN 1965 12586
MOOD OF CHOICE:
LEVEL
LR 13433
ANTENNA ROTATO
MODEL 9512
MOOD MASTER

THIS IS A VIRTUAL REALITY.

1. MAKE A LIST OF YOUR PERSONALITY TRAITS.
2. TAKE THOSE TRAITS AND EXAGGERATE OR EMBELLISH THEM. CREATE A CHARACTER (OR AVATAR) WITH THESE TRAITS AS SUPERPOWERS.
3. CREATE SEVERAL SUPERHERO ACCESORIES.

EXAMPES: HER EXCELLENT ORGANIZATIONAL SKILLS MAKE HER FULLY PREPARED FOR EVERY POTENTIAL CRISIS, HE REPELS ENEMIES WITH HIS LOVE OF GARLIC, SHE HAS A GREAT ABILITY TO FIND THINGS IN MESSY SPACES, HE IS A TIMING EXPERT.

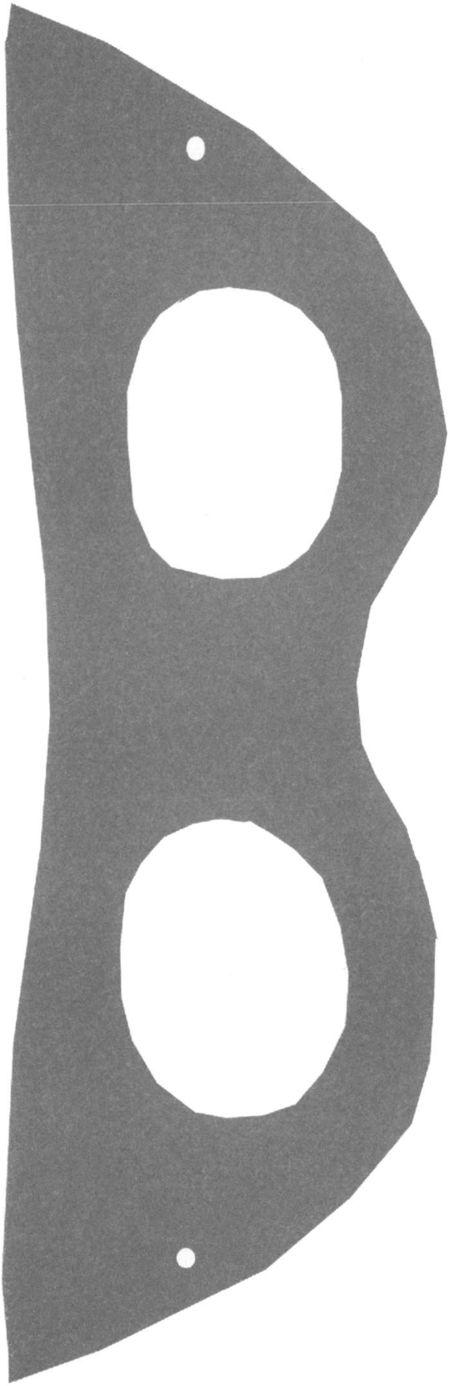

THIS IS A TOP SECRET DOCUMENT.

1. FIND A DICTIONARY.
2. WRITE A MESSAGE USING THIS CODE.
3. CUT THE CODE OUT AND HIDE IT SOMEWHERE IN <u>THIS IS NOT A BOOK</u>.
4. GIVE IT TO A FRIEND TO SOLVE.

<u>N + 7</u>

REPLACE EVERY NOUN IN A TEXT WITH THE NOUN SEVEN ENTRIES AFTER IT IN A DICTIONARY. THE MORE NOUNS YOU USE, THE MORE CRYPTIC IT WILL BE.

NAME
NOM
CLASSIFIED

No. N + 7

THIS IS AN EXCERPT FROM *another book*.

1. PULL A BOOK OFF YOUR BOOKSHELF (OR ONE AT A LIBRARY).
2. OPEN IT TO A RANDOM PAGE.
3. WRITE THE FIRST SENTENCE YOU SEE HERE.

111

subject:

THIS IS AN **EXCUSE** TO AVOID OTHER THINGS.

WRITE A LIST OF THINGS YOU WOULD LIKE TO AVOID HERE.

THIS IS AN INTERVIEW.

WHAT IS YOUR FULL NAME?

WHAT IS YOUR FAVORITE THING TO EAT?

DESCRIBE THE TASTE OF YOUR FAVORITE FO
WITHOUT COMPARING IT TO OTHER FOODS.

WHAT ARE YOUR FAVORITE THINGS TO DO?

WHO ARE YOUR FAVORITE PEOPLE?

WHAT WAS YOUR FAVORITE THING TO DO WHEN YOU WERE REALLY LITTLE?

DESCRIBE YOUR FAVORITE OUTFIT.

WHERE DO YOU SEE YOURSELF IN FIVE YEARS?

THIS IS A NETWORK.

CREATE AN ARRANGEMENT OF INTERSECTING LINES GOING EVERY WHICH WAY.

THIS IS A
PUBLIC SPACE.
INVITE PEOPLE TO ADD SOMETHING TO THIS PAGE.

IS IS AN **ITINERARY.**

GO TO THE CLOSEST PARK.

SPEND 10 MINUTES LOOKING AT THE SKY. WHAT DO YOU SEE?

. DOCUMENT YOURSELF STANDING UNDER A TREE (PHOTO, DRAWING, ETC.).

4. ARRANGE SOMETHING YOU FIND INTO A CIRCLE (LEAVES, STONES, ETC.).

5. LIST THE NUMBER OF PEOPLE YOU SEE.

. LEAVE SOMETHING OF YOURS IN A SECRET LOCATION.

THIS IS A WINDOW.

1. CUT OUT HOLE.
2. PLACE IN FRONT OF DESIRED VIEW.
3. SIT.

CUT OUT

THIS IS A **MOMENT IN TIME.**

THIS DAY WILL NEVER HAPPEN AGAIN.
DOCUMENT ITS PASSING.

THIS IS AN UNDERGROUND ORGANIZATION.

1. GO TO WWW.THISISNOTABOOK.ORG.
2. ENTER THIS CODE: JTZ5261.
3. RECEIVE YOUR MISSION.

THIS IS A MATERIAL.

CONDUCT SOME EXPERIMENTS TO UNCOVER THE PROPERTIES OF THIS PAGE (PAPER). MAKE A LIST AND TEST ALL OF THE THINGS YOU CAN DO TO IT. WHAT HAPPENS WHEN YOU ADD THINGS (SUBSTANCES) TO IT?

THIS IS A

PORTABLE HOLE/PORTAL.

MAKES THINGS DISAPPEAR AT WILL.

1. CUT OUT.
2. AFFIX THE HOLE TO ANY SURFACE.
3. USE.

IF YOU COULD BE ANYWHERE YOU WANT RIGHT NOW, WHERE WOULD IT BE?

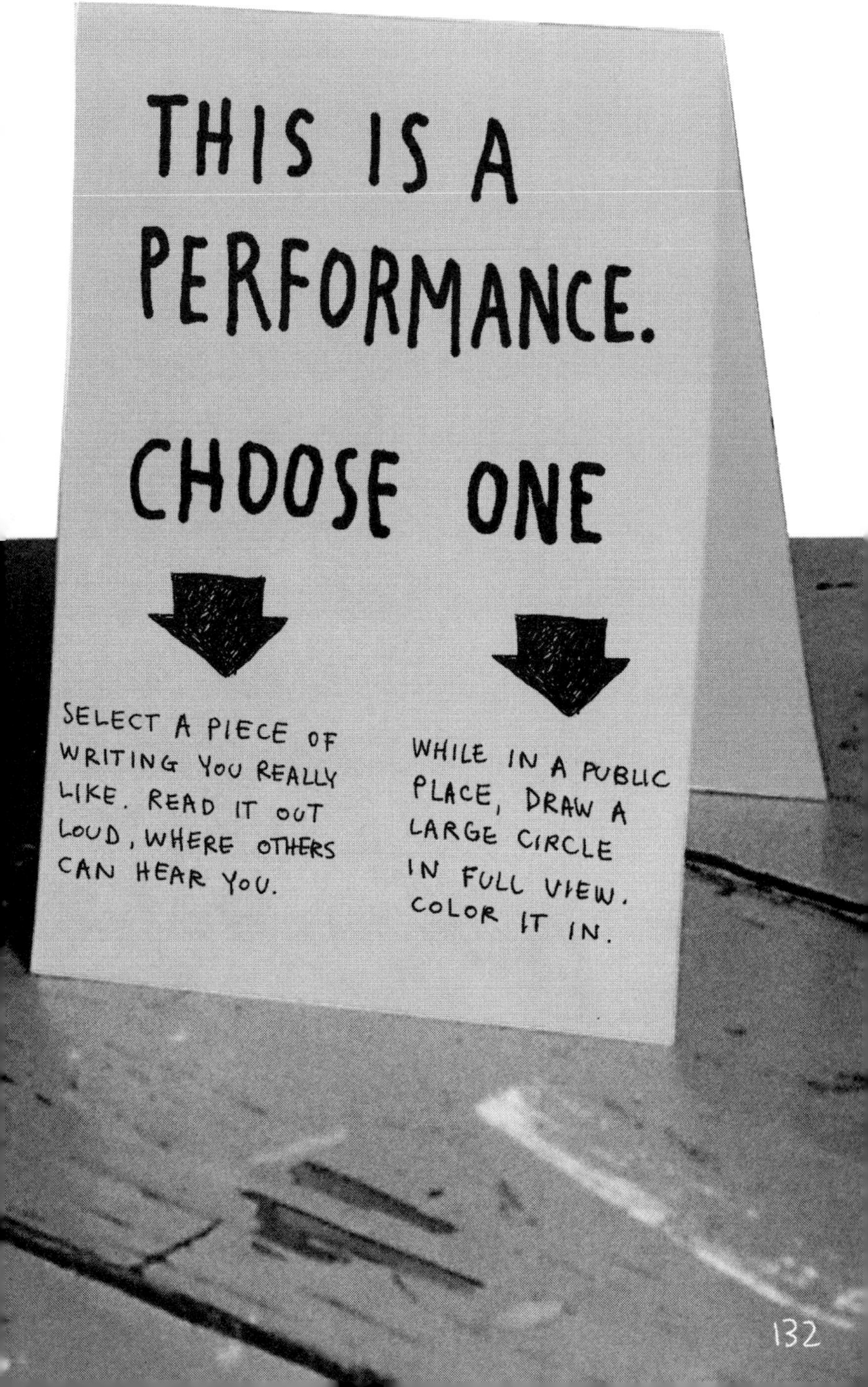
THIS IS A
PERFORMANCE.
CHOOSE ONE
SELECT A PIECE OF WRITING YOU REALLY LIKE. READ IT OUT LOUD, WHERE OTHERS CAN HEAR YOU.
WHILE IN A PUBLIC PLACE, DRAW A LARGE CIRCLE IN FULL VIEW. COLOR IT IN.

THIS IS A MULTIDIRECTIONAL UNIT.

1. GO TO A PLACE YOU WOULD LIKE TO EXPLORE.
2. OPEN THIS IS NOT A BOOK FLAT.
3. PLACE ON GROUND (OR FLOOR). SPIN.*
4. MOVE IN THE DIRECTION OF THE ARROW.
5. REPEAT WHENEVER A CHOICE OF DIRECTION PRESENTS ITSELF (E.G., INTERSECTION).

* IF SURFACE DOES NOT ALLOW SPINNING, PLACE THIS IS NOT A BOOK ON A LARGE PIECE OF CARDBOARD

GO THIS
WAY

135

THIS IS AN INVENTORY OF YOUR THINGS.

1. MAKE A LIST OF ITEMS YOU OWN.
2. BESIDE EACH ITEM PUT THE QUANTITY OF ITEMS (I.E., BOOKS: 432, PANTS: 4).

THIS IS A CELEBRATION

CREATE A HOMEMADE CELEBRATION USING WHATEVER YOU HAVE AROUND YOU.

1. COME UP WITH SOME KIND OF THEME.
2. MAKE A FESTIVE MEAL, DISH, OR DESSERT.
3. PLAY MUSIC YOU LIKE.
4. A SPECIAL OUTFIT OR COSTUME ALWAYS HELPS. INVITE FRIENDS.
5. USING MAGAZINES, NEWSPAPERS, OR COLORED PAPER, CUT OUT A NUMBER OF TRIANGLES AND ATTACH TO STRING FOR A BANNER.

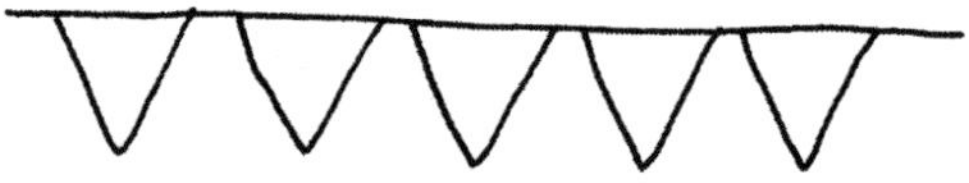

THIS IS A PLATE.

PLACE YOUR DINNER HERE.

THIS IS A PLOT TO RULE THE WORLD.

IF I ______________ COULD RULE THE WORLD,
(YOUR NAME HERE)
I WOULD MAKE THE FOLLOWING CHANGES

WORLD LEADER

THIS IS A

COME UP WITH 50 DIFFERENT WAYS THIS IS NOT A BOOK COULD BE USED AS A TOOL OR UTENSIL OF SOME KIND.

TOOL.

TOOL |TOŌL|

NOUN

A DEVICE OR IMPLEMENT, ESP. ONE HELD IN THE HAND, USED TO CARRY OUT A PARTICULAR FUNCTION.

THIS IS A CUSTOMIZABLE OBJECT.

ADD YOUR OWN FEATURES TO THIS IS NOT A BOOK. SOME IDEAS: COLOR IN SOME PAGES, SHAPE THE PAGES WITH SCISSORS, ADD STRIPES, GLUE IN ENVELOPES FOR COLLECTING THINGS, ADD AN ELASTIC BAND TO HOLD IT CLOSED, MAKE YOUR OWN BOOKMARK, WRITE NOTES IN BLANK SPACES, FOLD DOWN CORNERS, COLOR THE EDGES OF THE PAGES, ADD A GRID, ADD A MAP OF YOUR CITY, ADD LINES, ADD STICKERS, MAKE SOME KIND OF CARRYING CASE FOR IT.

THIS OBJECT BELONGS TO:

....

....

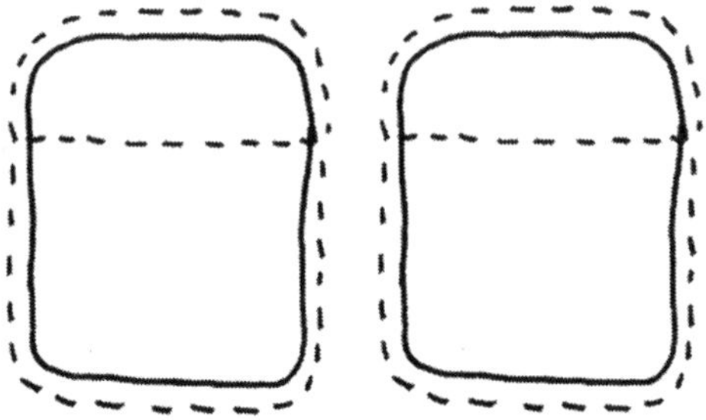

HERE ARE SOME NOTE TABS FOR YOU TO CUT OUT AND GLUE ON.

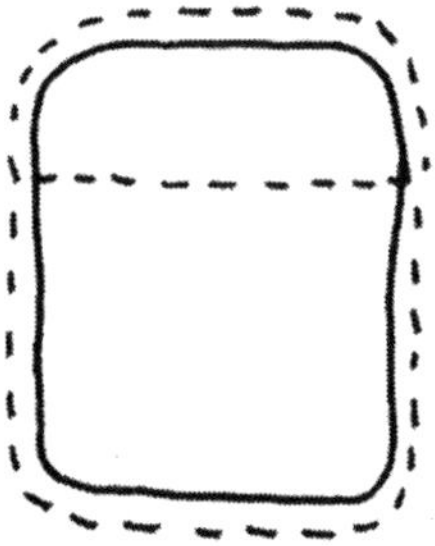

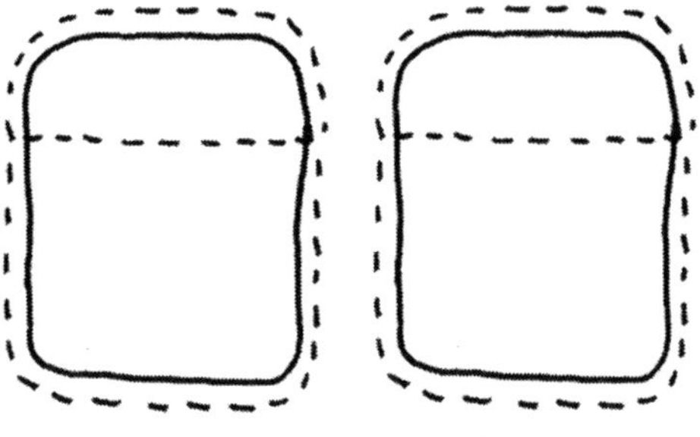

CUSTOMIZED BY: ____________.

BOOKMARK

THIS IS A **SYSTEM**. CHOOSE ONE WORD FROM EACH PAGE OF <u>THIS IS NOT A BOOK</u> TO FORM A VERY LONG SENTENCE.

THIS IS **MAIL.**

CUT OUT, GLUE ONTO CARDBOARD, AND MAIL TO A FRIEND.

THIS IS NOT A BOOK.
THIS IS A POSTCARD.

THIS IS A

DO SOMETHING TO THIS PAGE TO MAKE IT SO PEOPLE WILL WANT TO AVOID IT.

THIS IS A FORM OF MOVEMENT.

DOCUMENT SOME KIND OF MOVEMENT HERE (E.G., TAPPING WITH A PEN, RUNNING AND JUMPING WITH A PENCIL, WALKING, ETC.).

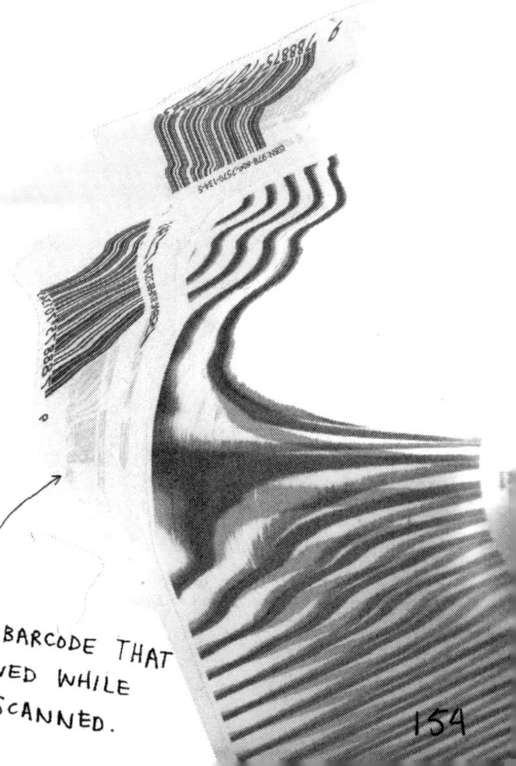

A UPC BARCODE THAT WAS MOVED WHILE BEING SCANNED.

155

THIS IS A RANDOM ADVENTURE.

1. GO OUTSIDE.

2. WALK UNTIL YOU SEE SOMETHING RED.

3. TAKE TEN STEPS.

4. LOOK DOWN AT YOUR FEET AND DESCRIBE WHAT YOU SEE IN DETAIL.

THIS IS A DREAM CATCHER.

PUT THIS IS NOT A BOOK NEXT TO YOU WHILE YOU ARE SLEEPING AND YOUR DREAMS WILL STICK TO THE PAGES. (YOU MAY HAVE TO WRITE THEM DOWN RIGHT HERE WHEN YOU WAKE UP.) ⟶

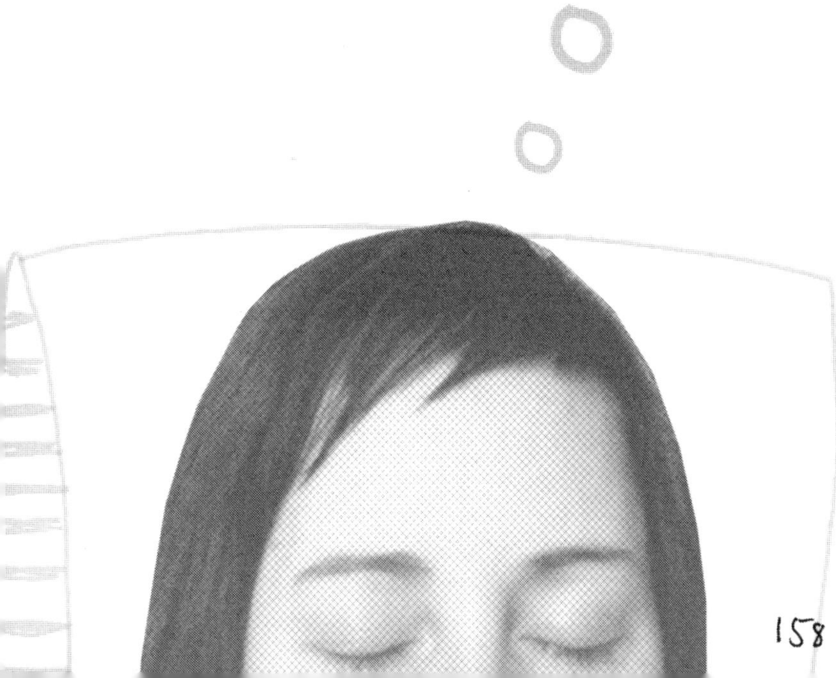

THIS IS A **SCHOOL.**

IF YOU COULD TEACH <u>ANY</u> CLASS,
WHAT WOULD IT BE?

DESCRIBE THE CURRICULUM, FIELD TRIPS,
GUEST SPEAKERS, ETC.

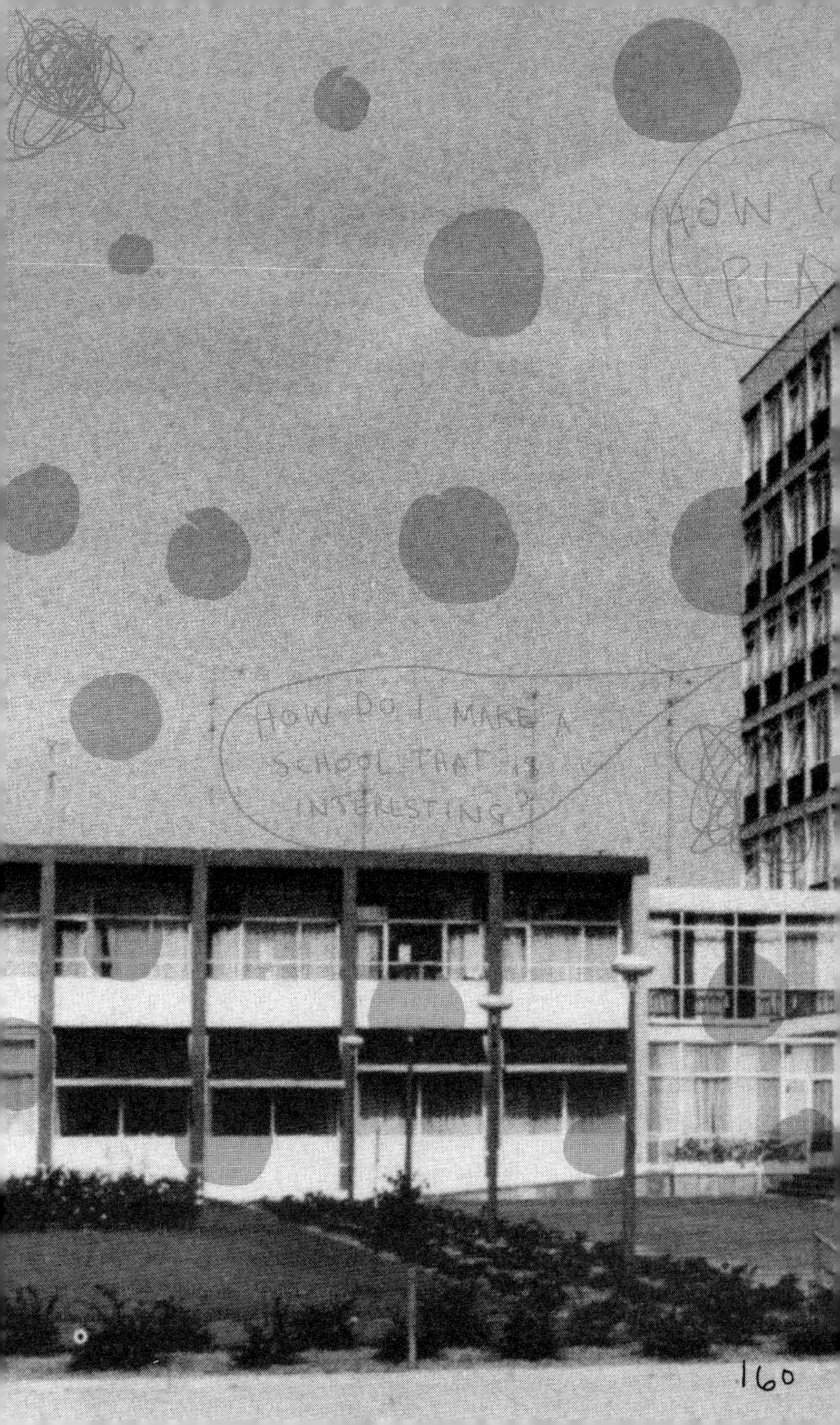
HOW DO I MAKE A SCHOOL THAT IS INTERESTING?

THIS IS AN **INSTRUMENT.**

1. USING <u>THIS IS NOT A BOOK</u> AS A SOURCE, COME UP WITH AS MANY DIFFERENT SOUNDS AS YOU CAN (E.G. FLIP THE PAGES, BANG IT, ETC.).
2. DOCUMENT YOUR METHODS HERE.

THIS IS A SENSORY STIMULATION UNIT.

1. COLLECT FIVE THINGS, ONE FOR EACH SENSE.
2. AFFIX THEM HERE.

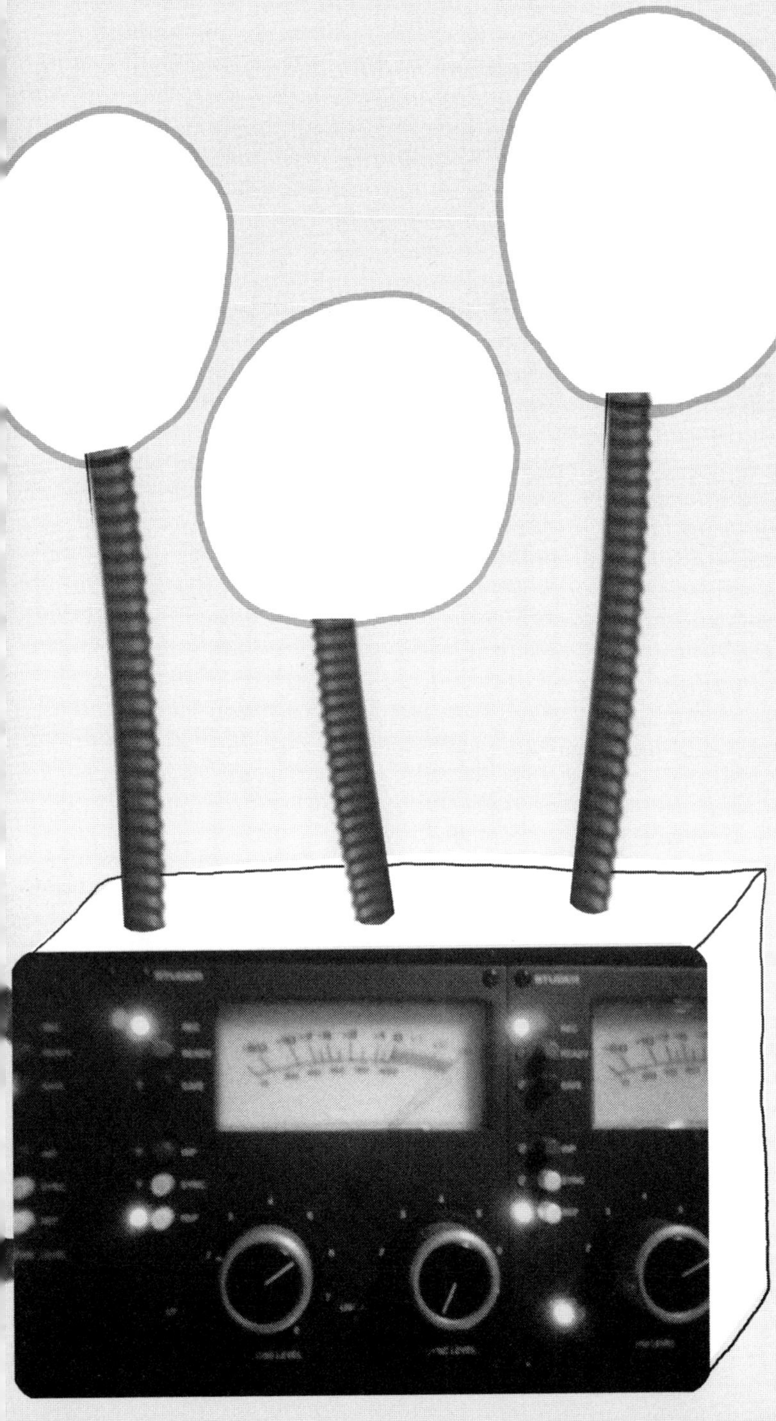

HIS IS AN OUTLET.

ENT ABOUT THINGS THAT ARE BOTHERING YOU HERE.

(IF YOU'RE REALLY MAD YOU MIGHT WANT TO SCRIBBLE UNCONTROLLABLY.)

167

THIS IS A SCULPTURE.

1. USING THIS PAGE CREATE A THREE-DIMENSIONAL OBJECT. YOU MAY COLOR OR ALTER THE PAGE ANY WAY YOU WISH.
2. CREATE A TAG FOR YOUR SCULPTURE.
3. EXHIBIT IT SOMEWHERE.

THIS IS A GAME.

1. PLAYERS TAKE TURNS PLACLNG <u>THIS IS NOT A BOOK</u> IN A DIFFERENT LOCATION FOR EACH ROUND.

2. THERE ARE FIVE ROUNDS. IN EACH ROUND PLAYERS TAKE TURNS RETRIEVING THIS IS NOT A BOOK ACCORDING TO THE REQUIREMENTS ON THE LIST.

OPTIONAL: TIME EACH ROUND. GIVE EACH PLAYER TWO MINUTES.

CREATE FIVE MORE REQUIREMENTS (ROUNDS).

ROUND ONE: RETRIEVE THIS IS NOT A BOOK WITH EYES SHUT.

ROUND TWO: RETRIEVE THIS IS NOT A BOOK WITH NO HANDS.

ROUND THREE: CONVINCE A THIRD PARTY TO RETRIEVE THIS IS NOT A BOOK FOR YOU.

ROUND FOUR: RETRIEVE THIS IS NOT A BOOK WHILE STANDING ON ONE LEG.

ROUND FIVE: RETRIEVE THIS IS NOT A BOOK USING A TOOL OR UTENSIL.

THIS IS A CURRENCY.

USE THIS MONEY TO BEGIN YOUR OWN ECONOMY AND BARTER SYSTEM.

TRADE THIS PAGE FOR ANOTHER ITEM OF EQUAL OR GREATER VALUE.

DRAW YOUR OWN VERSION OF MONEY.

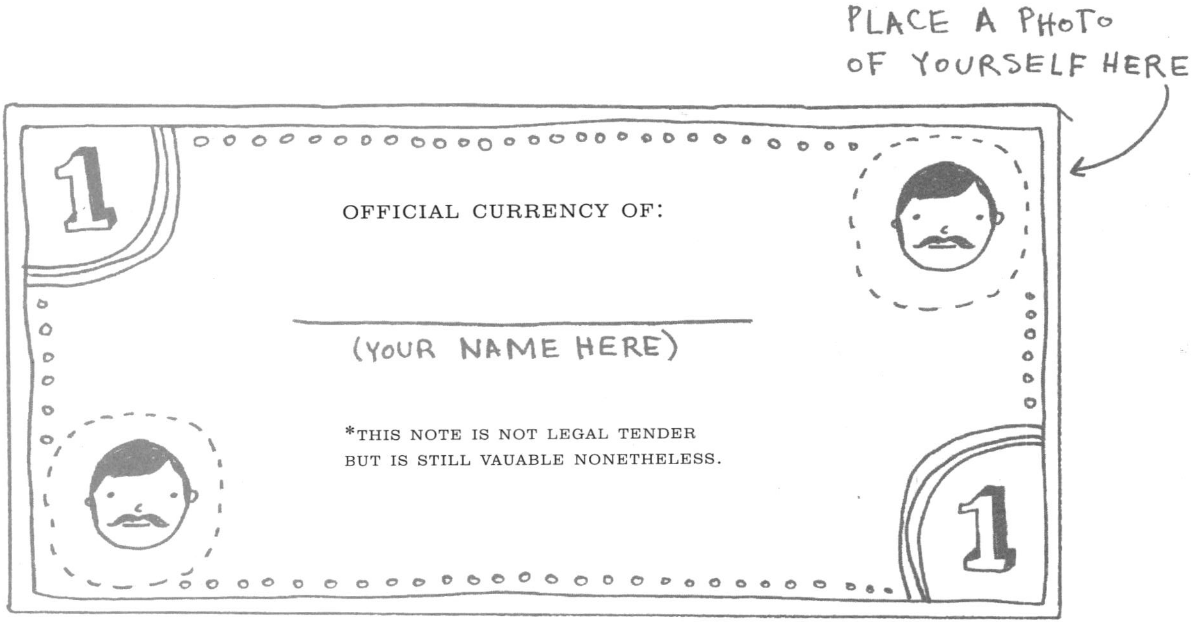
PLACE A PHOTO OF YOURSELF HERE
1
OFFICIAL CURRENCY OF:
(YOUR NAME HERE)
*THIS NOTE IS NOT LEGAL TENDER
BUT IS STILL VAUABLE NONETHELESS.
1

THIS IS A **PUZZLE**.

CAN YOU MAKE A HOLE IN THIS PAGE THAT A PERSON CAN PASS THROUGH?

FIND THE ANSWER AT WWW.THISISNOTABOOK.ORG.

THIS IS A STRUCTURE.

1. CREATE A STRUCTURE OF SOME KIND COMBINING <u>THIS IS NOT A BOOK</u> WITH OTHER OBJECTS.
2. DOCUMENT IT SOMEHOW.

THIS IS A KIT FOR ATTENDIN BORING EVENTS.

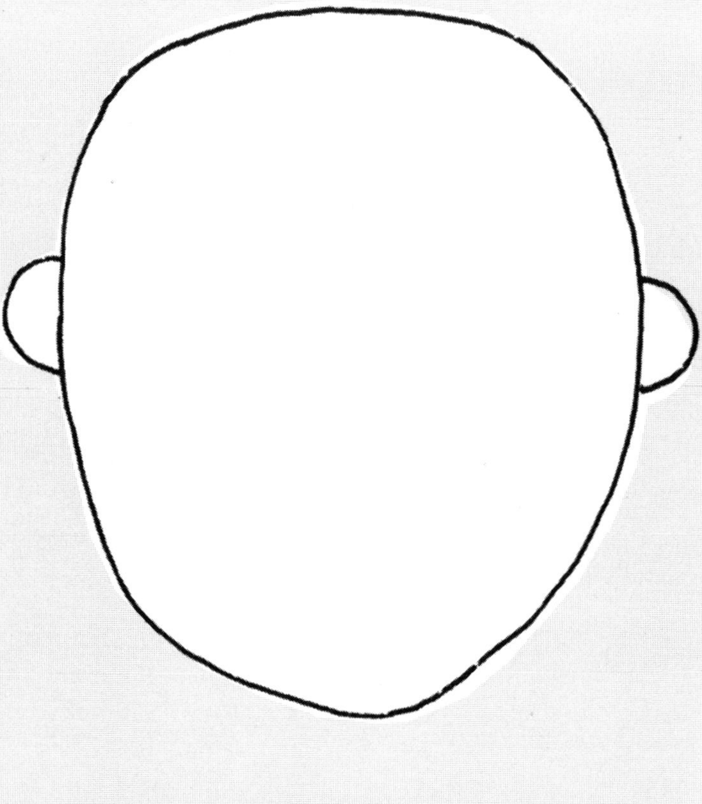

DRAW A FUNNY FACE.

ND THESE WORDS AND CIRCLE THEM.

L	U	F	T	N	E	V	E	N	U	D
E	R	U	X	T	E	D	F	E	N	E
N	O	B	T	I	R	E	D	N	E	A
D	U	L	L	E	T	R	E	X	X	Y
T	E	A	M	S	S	M	L	O	C	R
L	A	N	A	B	I	V	A	P	I	D
R	I	D	S	I	G	R	T	W	T	M
L	I	F	E	L	E	S	S	O	I	T
E	T	S	U	L	K	C	A	L	N	S
R	E	A	M	D	V	M	I	G	G	L

UNEVENTFUL
DULL
BLAND
BANAL
LIFELESS
UNEXCITING
DRY
STALE
MUNDANE
TIRED
LACKLUSTER

WRITE A LIST OF
TEN THINGS YOU
CAN SEE RIGHT NOW.

179

THIS IS A *declaration.*

CARVE SOMETHING ONTO THIS TREE.

THIS IS A MIRROR.

CREATE A SELF PORTRAIT BY DOCUMENTING THE THINGS THAT DEFINE YOU (CLOTHING, FOOD, HOBBIES, ETC.). YOU CAN DRAW, PHOTOGRAPH, OR WRITE ABOUT THEM HERE.

THIS IS A COLLECTION
OF FOUND THINGS.
1. PLACE SOME THINGS THAT YOU FIND ON EACH SHELF.
2. WRITE NOTES ABOUT HOW THEY ARE MAGICA

185

THIS IS A CONUNDRUM.

THIS IS AN UNUSUAL PARAGRAPH. IT IS A CONUNDRUM FOR YOU TO SORT OUT. HOW QUICKLY CAN YOU FIND OUT WHAT IS SO UNCOMMON ABOUT IT? IT LOOKS SO ORDINARY THAT YOU MAY THINK NOTHING IS ODD ABOUT IT, UNTIL YOU ACTUALLY MATCH IT AGAINST MOST PARAGRAPHS THIS LONG. IF YOU PUT YOUR MIND TO IT AND STUDY IT HARD, YOU WILL FIND OUT. NOBODY MAY ASSIST YOU — DO IT WITHOUT ANY COACHING. GO TO WORK AND TRY YOUR SKILL AT FIGURING IT OUT. GOOD LUCK!

FIND THE ANSWER AT WWW.THISISNOTABOOK.ORG.

THIS IS A FORTUNE TELLER.

1. CUT OUT SQUARES.
2. ASK A YES OR NO QUESTION.
3. CLOSE EYES AND PICK A SQUARE FOR YOUR ANSWER.

YES

THIS IS A MYSTERY

MAYBE

YOU'RE ON TO SOMETHING

TRY AGAIN

NO

189

THIS IS A MYSTERY.

PAGE NUMBER 42 IS MISSING. WHAT DO YOU THINK HAPPENED TO IT? WRITE YOUR POSTULATIONS HERE. SUBMIT THEM TO WWW.THISISNOTABOOK.ORG.

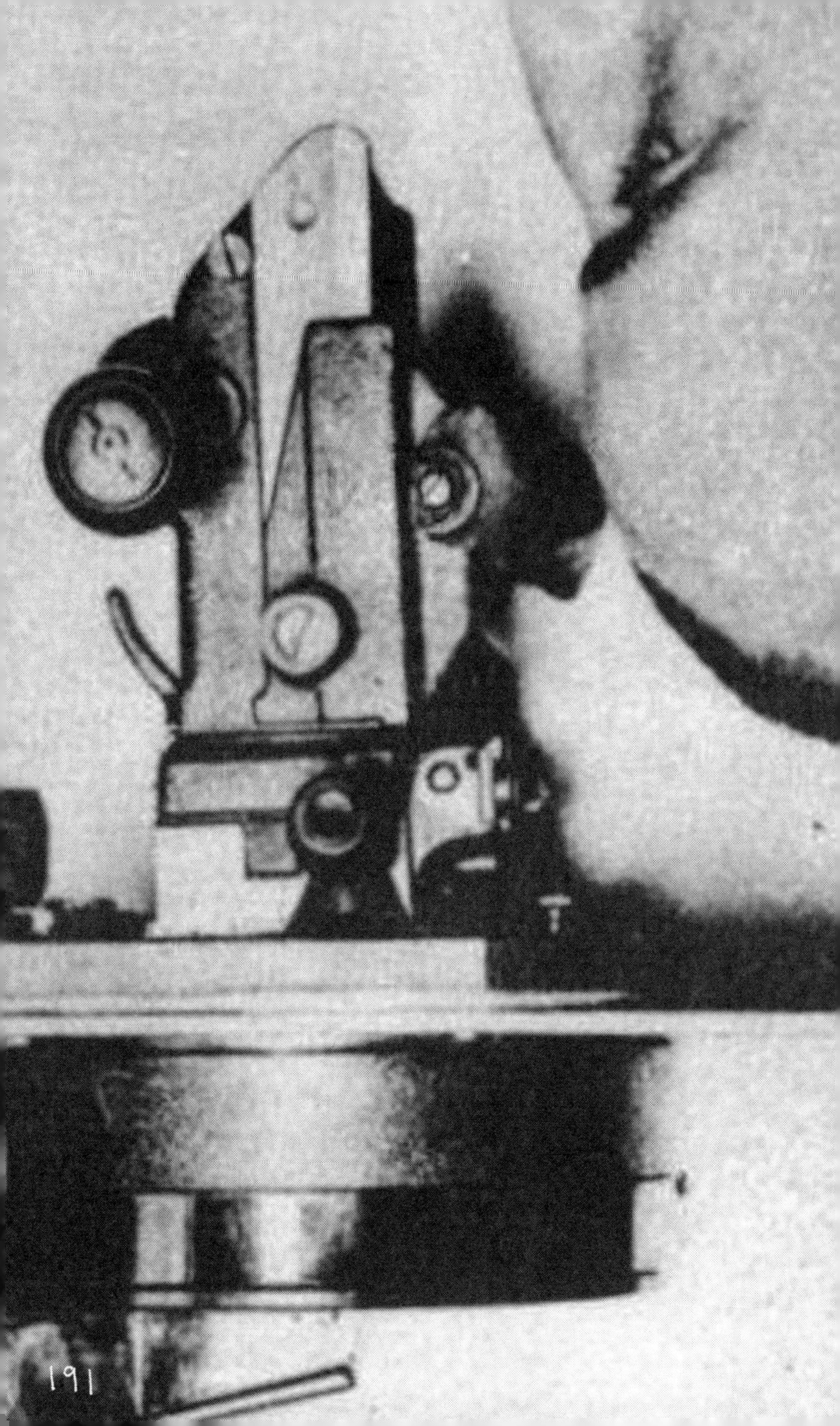
191

THIS IS A PARALLEL UNIVERSE.

WHAT WOULD YOUR WORLD BE LIKE
IF EVERYTHING WAS THE OPPOSITE
OF WHAT IT IS NOW?

THIS IS AN ACCIDENT.

CHOOSE ONE OF THE FOLLOWING:

1. PLACE A FEW DROPS OF INK ON THE PAGE AND BLOW WITH A STRAW.
2. CUT A BUNCH OF SMALL SHAPES OUT OF COLORED PAPER. DROP THEM ONTO THE PAGE AND GLUE THEM WHERE THEY LAND.
3. PLACE <u>THIS IS NOT A BOOK</u> ON THE FLOOR AND DROP INK ONTO IT WHILE STANDING.

THIS IS A TRAP.

DO SOMETHING OR WRITE SOMETHING THAT WILL MAKE SOMEONE ELSE WANT TO PICK UP THIS IS NOT A BOOK.

THIS IS A STREAM OF CONSCIOUSNESS
WHAT ARE YOU THI
ABOUT RIGHT NOW?

THIS IS A LANDSCAPE.

FIND A WAY TO MAKE THIS PAGE BLEND COMPLETELY WITH OR FIT INTO A ROOM OR LANDSCAPE OF YOUR CHOOSING.

THIS IS A CHANCE OPERATION.

1. CUT OUT GRID.
2. PLACE IN A BOWL OR CONTAINER.
3. PICK ONE.
4. FOLLOW INSTRUCTIONS.
5. REPEAT.

OLOR A AGE BLACK.	DESCRIBE YOURSELF WITHOUT USING WORDS.	RECORD AN OVERHEARD CONVERSATION.
EMOVE PAGE.	HIDE <u>THIS IS NOT A BOOK</u> FOR A WEEK.	CREATE AN APPENDAGE FOR <u>THIS IS NOT A BOOK</u>.
OVER A AGE WITH INES.	HAVE A FRIEND CHOOSE WHAT PAGE YOU DO NEXT.	WRITE DOWN EVERYTHING IN YOUR HEAD RIGHT NOW.
MAKE A JIGSAW PUZZLE OUT OF PAPER.	TRANSFORM SOME GARBAGE.	LIST ALL OF THE SOUNDS YOU HEAR.

203

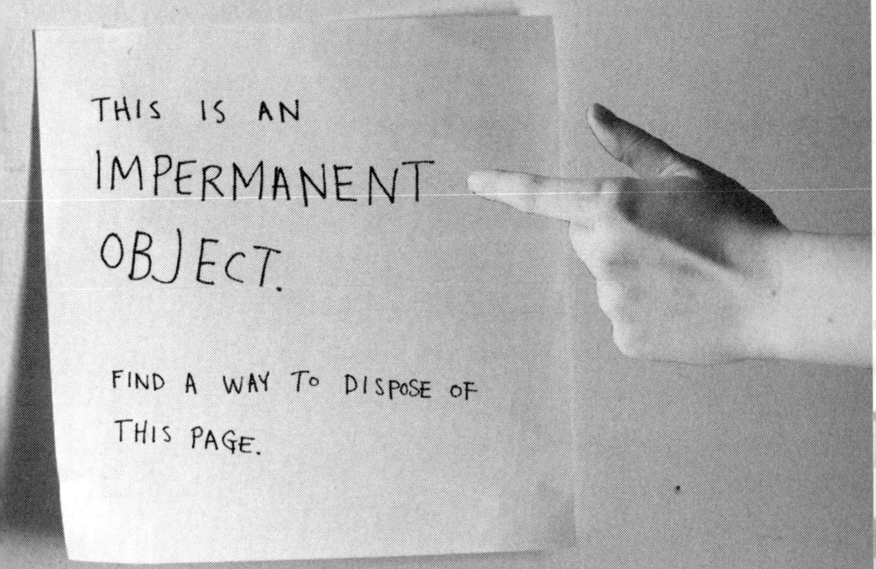
THIS IS AN
IMPERMANENT
OBJECT.
FIND A WAY TO DISPOSE OF
THIS PAGE.

THIS IS A REPETITIVE MOTION.

MAKE THE SAME REPETITIVE MARKINGS TO THE ENTIRE PAGE (E.G., TINY SQUARES, DASHES).

THIS IS A SOUVENIR
(OF YOUR TIME SPENT ON THE PLANET).
MAKE A LIST OF THINGS YOU MOST ENJOY ABOUT BEING HERE.

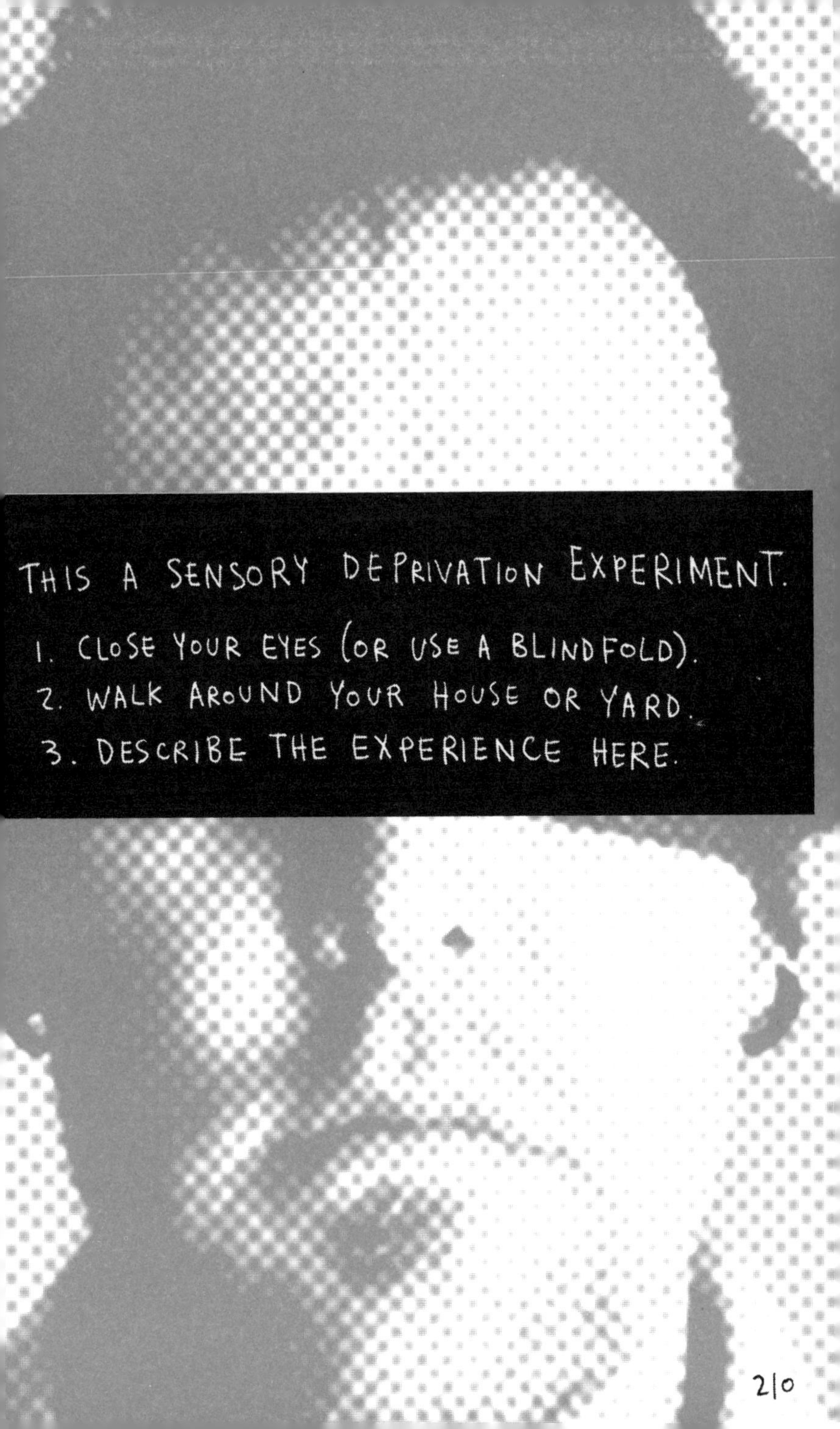

THIS A SENSORY DEPRIVATION EXPERIMENT.

1. CLOSE YOUR EYES (OR USE A BLINDFOLD).
2. WALK AROUND YOUR HOUSE OR YARD.
3. DESCRIBE THE EXPERIENCE HERE.

THIS IS A WALL (OR PRIVATE S

1. OPEN THIS IS NOT A BOOK, STAND IT UP LIKE THIS.
2. USE IN PUBLIC WHEN A LITTLE PRIVACY IS NEEDED.
3. YOU MAY CUT A HOLE HERE TO SPY IN SOME WAY.

THIS IS A
WALL.

THIS IS A LANGUAGE.

DOCUMENT A JOURNEY USING THE CODES BELOW.
ADD YOUR OWN CODES. TELL A STORY.

THIS IS A COLLABORATION

1. ASSIGN SOMEONE A GUEST PASS FOR THIS PAGE.
2. INSTRUCT THEM TO ALTER IT IN ANY WAY THEY WISH.

GUEST

NAME:______________________________

VISITING:____________________________

DATE: TIME IN: TIME OUT:

THIS IS A REPRODUCTION.

1. FILL IN THIS SQUARE WITH PENCIL OR CHARCOAL.
2. CUT ALONG DOTTED LINE. FOLD PAGE LIKE THIS.
3. DRAW SOMETHING. LIFT TO SEE COPY.

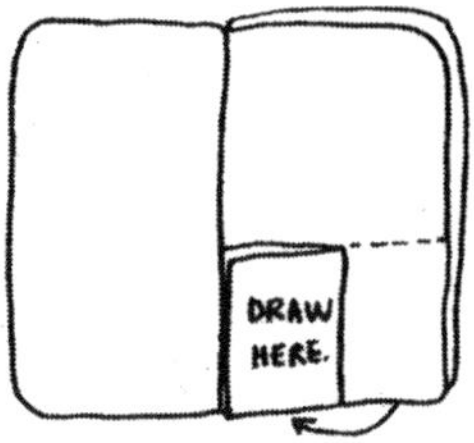

FOLD HERE

PENCIL OR CHARCOAL GOES HERE.

THIS IS A LIST OF OTHER THINGS
THIS IS NOT A BOOK COULD BE.
COME UP WITH YOUR OWN VERSIONS
OF WHAT THEY MIGHT LOOK LIKE.

A PUPPET
A PROTEST
A REVOLUTION
A FORM OF TECHNOLOGY
AN ANSWER TO A QUESTION
A DEBATE
A MICROCOSM
A QUIZ
A SCIENCE EXPERIMENT
A COMMAND
A DIVERSION
A RED HERRING
AN ARTIFICE
A SHIFT IN PERCEPTION
AN IDEOLOGY
A MONUMENT
A MEME
A NEIGHBORHOOD

A TIMELINE
A SPECTACLE
A GIFT
A PRACTICAL JOKE
A MECHANISM
A TIME CAPSULE
A DATABASE
A RUMOR
AN INTERACTION
A CONFESSION
A SEAT
AN ARTICLE OF CLOTHING
THE CENTER OF THE UNIVERSE
AN EXTRAORDINARY EVENT
A DEMONSTRATION OF GRAVITY
A FAKE
AN OUTLINE

NOTES:

RANDOM OCCURRENCE IS AN HOMAGE TO MARCEL DUCHAMP.

WINDOW IS AN HOMAGE TO YOKO ONO.

CHANCE OPERATION IS AN HOMAGE TO JOHN CAGE.

CONUNDRUM AND TOP SECRET DOCUMENT ARE AN HOMAGE TO THE OULIPO GROUP.

BUREAUCRACY IS AN HOMAGE TO JOSÉ SARAMAGO.

VOYAGE IS AN HOMAGE TO BAS JAN ADER.

KERI SMITH IS THE AUTHOR OF SEVERAL BOOKS INCLUDING WRECK THIS JOURNAL AND HOW TO BE AN EXPLORER OF THE WORLD: PORTABLE ~~ART~~/ LIFE MUSEUM.

READ MORE AT WWW.KERISMITH.COM.

MESS

THE MANUAL OF ACCIDENTS AND MISTAKES

Keri Smith

PENGUIN BOOKS

PENGUIN BOOKS

Published by the Penguin Group
Penguin Books Ltd, 80 Strand, London WC2R ORL, England
Penguin Group (USA) Inc., 375 Hudson Street, New York, New York 10014, USA
Penguin Group (Canada), 90 Eglinton Avenue East, Suite 700, Toronto, Ontario, Canada M4P 2Y3
(a division of Pearson Penguin Canada Inc.)
Penguin Ireland, 25 St Stephen's Green, Dublin 2, Ireland (a division of Penguin Books Ltd)
Penguin Group (Australia), 250 Camberwell Road, Camberwell, Victoria 3124, Australia
(a division of Pearson Australia Group Pty Ltd)
Penguin Books India Pvt Ltd, 11 Community Centre, Panchsheel Park, New Delhi – 110 017, India
Penguin Group (NZ), 67 Apollo Drive, Rosedale, North Shore 0632, New Zealand
(a division of Pearson New Zealand Ltd)
Penguin Books (South Africa) (Pty) Ltd, 24 Sturdee Avenue, Rosebank,
Johannesburg 2196, South Africa

Penguin Books Ltd, Registered Offices: 80 Strand, London WC2R ORL, England

www.penguin.com

First published in the USA by Penguin Group (USA) Inc., 2010
First published in Great Britain by Penguin Books 2010
009

Printed in Great Britain by Clays Ltd, St Ives plc

978–1–846–14447–9

WARNING:

DO NOT TRY TO MAKE SOMETHING BEAUTIFUL. DO NOT THROW THIS BOOK OUT WHEN YOU DISLIKE A PAGE YOU CREATED. DO NOT PLAY IT SAFE. DO NOT WORRY ABOUT LEGIBILITY. DO HAVE FUN. DO GET DIRTY. DO TRY SOMETHING YOU'VE NEVER TRIED BEFORE. DON'T THINK TOO MUCH. (IT ALWAYS HELPS TO QUIET THE MIND.)

WRITE YOUR OWN INTRO

Note: You may choose to read the following eight-page introduction, or you can choose to skip it and write your own version in the space on the left. You may also wish to begin the exercises immediately.

INTRODUCTION

A few years ago I became fascinated by the work of Dutch-born artist Bas Jan Ader. The first piece I saw of his was the video "Broken Fall," which depicts a man hanging precariously by his hands from a high tree branch, swinging back and forth over a small creek. As the branch bobs and sways, I found myself waiting for the inevitable. Amid the tension of waiting, I also found myself smiling and laughing uncontrollably. And then it happens. The man plunges into the creek and crawls up the side of the bank, the whole thing lasting a mere 1 minute, 44 seconds.

Ader often dealt with the subject of gravity—various methods of falling, or dropping things. It seems completely ridiculous, and this is what I love about it. It is absurd, brilliantly simple, and completely serious at the same time.

In the film, there is an interview with an old Dutch sailor that sums up Ader's work perfectly. He speaks indirectly about the process of improvisation, but the connection I made from it is that the point of Ader's "falls" is not the falling but the moment (1/10th of a second) where he makes the decision to let go. That is the moment of transcendence when you leave everything behind and leap into the unknown.

As improvisers, artists, or experimenters, we are trying to re-create that moment–when you leave everything behind and leap into the unknown. Because we've done it before and it's addictive–that seductive release, a sense of giddyness mixed with fear. For an instant you get a feeling that you are really doing something worthwhile, living out on the edge of something big, yet unnamable. A kind of opening (with all the vulnerability that comes with that).

We all know what it feels like to fall, but how many of us have experimented with gravity as a medium? Isn't falling or breaking things something we only do by accident? What does it feel like to throw yourself off balance on purpose?

Definition of "mistake" or "accident" (for the purposes of this book): *Happenings or occurrences by which the creator does not have complete control over the final outcome (end result) that result in conclusions the creator did not predict. We might also call them "experiments."*

During the course of working on this book, I realized that what I am really talking about when I speak of "mistakes" is improvisation. The process of improvising involves throwing ourselves off balance for a time, into a situation where we have to make decisions on the spot. Forced decision making puts us into a place where we have no choice but to accept what has occurred and then move on, to work with what exists. But it also pushes us into some places that we would not normally go. This to me is the purpose of this book: to participate in some situations where you have limited control and venture into territory that you would not normally go with the possibility of creating something completely new and different than what you might have done before.

DEREK BAILEY ON IMPROVISATION:

"A LOT OF IMPROVISERS FIND IMPROVISATION WORTHWHILE, I THINK, BECAUSE OF THE POSSIBILITIES. THINGS THAT CAN HAPPEN BUT PERHAPS RARELY DO. ONE OF THOSE THINGS IS THAT YOU ARE 'TAKEN OUT OF YOURSELF.' SOMETHING HAPPENS WHICH SO DISORIENTATES YOU THAT, FOR A TIME, WHICH MIGHT ONLY LAST A SECOND OR TWO, YOUR REACTIONS AND RESPONSES ARE NOT WHAT THEY NORMALLY WOULD BE. YOU CAN DO SOMETHING YOU DIDN'T REALIZE YOU WERE CAPABLE OF."

One of the biggest handicaps that occurs with both trained and untrained artists is a kind of reverential attitude toward making things "beautiful, accurate, and perfect." What is missing in this approach is a spontaneity or playful attitude with regard to materials and process. There is a lack of experimentation. In this approach the final product becomes more important than the process.

With the exercises in this book I would like to propose partaking in the experience and process of creating something with a total disregard of the outcome. Let's make the experience the thing. What if you were completely liberated from the final product?

SO, HOW DO YOU MAKE A MISTAKE ON PURPOSE?

It is my hope that by opening oneself up to the unknown at first in small ways (such as playing with materials), we begin to create a "habit" of experimentation. Slowly we become more accustomed to taking risks with our work. In time this can translate into bigger steps, both with creating a piece of artwork and in life. In this sense, whether it is really a mistake or not is irrelevant.

WHY WOULD YOU WANT TO DO THIS?

Contemplating and actively participating in imperfection (occasions where we open to failure) brings to us a freedom because it allows us to relax and enjoy the ebb and flow of life. Life does not always bring to us things that are "tidy." There is beauty to be found in the mess.

Messes can also be beneficial in presenting unexpected connections and juxtapositions. These often lead to new ideas, explorations, combinations, and solutions.

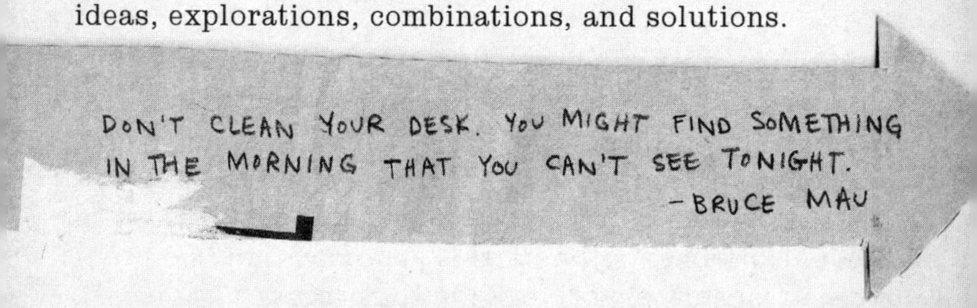
DON'T CLEAN YOUR DESK. YOU MIGHT FIND SOMETHING IN THE MORNING THAT YOU CAN'T SEE TONIGHT.
-BRUCE MAU

MISTAKES AND MESSES IN DIFFERENT CONTEXTS (WAYS OF APPROACHING IMPROVISATION):

-movement (getting lost, tripping, walking backwards, throwing)
-materials (cutting, dripping, dropping, crushing, decaying, etc.)
-writing (abolishing grammar and spelling)
-social interactions (speech, actions)

TECHNIQUES YOU WILL USE IN THIS BOOK

-serendipity (the effect by which one accidentally discovers something fortunate, especially while looking for something entirely unrelated)
-indeterminacy (work created using chance, luck, or magic)
-scarcity/excess of material
-improvisation/intuition
-play, exploring the qualities of materials
-deviance (straying from norms)
-misinterpretation
-interruptions, participating in an activity and seeing what happens when it is interrupted at different points (interruption methods can be random or planned)
-combining new ideas
-speed
-underestimation and overestimation
-subconscious thought
-détournement, a concept created by the Situationists, which is an alteration to an existing work that gives it a new meaning.

METHOD

The following exercises are designed to do two things:

1. To throw you into a place where you have little or no control over the outcome.
2. To work with a variety of materials in an exploratory fashion.

MATERIALS YOU MAY NEED:

scissors, pen, pencil, ink, water, some kind of water-based paint, charcoal, sticks, white glue, tape, crayons, paper, coffee, tea, juice, ice cream, sand paper, shovel, chalk, dictionary, stones, found photo, magazine or newspaper, paper bag, straw, elastic band, markers, bowl, pushpins, leaves, balloons, food, dirt, can, egg carton, toilet paper roll, plastic bags, cereal box, fabric, blue things, string, hammer, chalk, egg, paintbrush, cardboard, an eraser, a digital camera, a coin, dust, cocoa, flour, pin, iron, ash, gumption.

There is no such thing as a failed experiment, only experiments with unexpected outcomes.

–R. Buckminster Fuller

AND SO WE BEGIN . . .

1. While drawing a line, have someone bump this book.
2. Repeat numerous times.
Alternate: Draw a line while you are on the subway, in a car, on the bus, etc. Take notes on date, time, location.

1. Cover this page with something sticky (glue, honey, etc.).
2. Drop a powdery substance onto the page (cocoa, flour, etc.).
3. Blow off excess.

Drop some kind of colored liquid (ink, tea, coffee) here from a good height (at least five feet).

ERE IS MUCH BEAUTY TO BE FOUND IN DRIPS AND SPLOTCHES.

DO NOT STICK ANYTHING HERE. DO NOT SCRIBBLE ON THIS PAGE. DO NOT COVER UP THIS TYPE. DO NOT TOUCH THIS PAGE WITH DIRTY HANDS. DO NOT READ THIS PAGE WHILE EATING. DO NOT WALK ON THIS PAGE WITH YOUR SHOES. DO NOT RUB THIS PAGE WITH DIRT. DO NOT FOLD DOWN THE CORNERS OF THIS PAGE. DO NOT WRITE NOTES TO YOUR FRIENDS HERE. DO NOT TEAR THIS PAGE. DO NOT GET THIS PAGE WET. DO NOT LET A FRIEND WRITE ON THIS PAGE. DO NOT TRY TO COVER UP THIS PAGE.

Break the rules.

1. Rub some kind of pigment on your elbows (dirt, paint, ash, etc.).
2. Lean here.

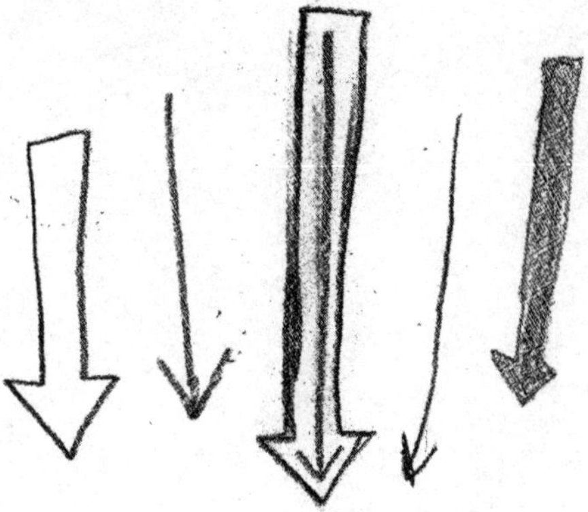

1. Cut pieces of white paper into tiny strips (1/8 inch X 1 inch).
2. Coat black page with white glue.
3. Drop the strips one at a time from a good height.
4. Press the strips down where they landed so they stick to the page.

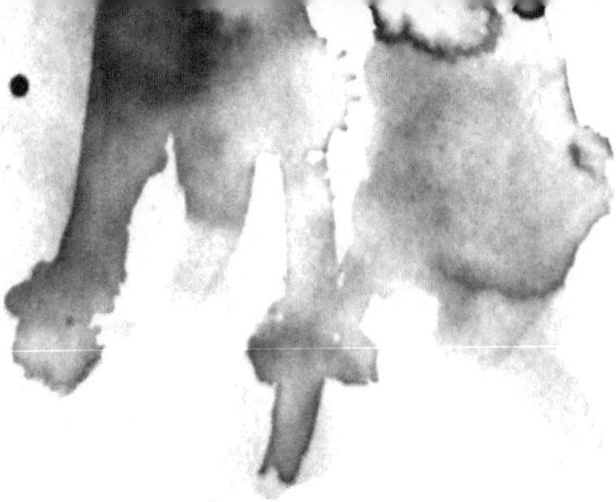

1. Drip some kind of colored liquid here (ink, watercolor, tea, juice, etc.).
2. Move the book so that it runs in all directions.
3. Let dry.

Alternate: Blow liquid with a straw (see image on last page), or fold page to create a symmetrical inkblot.

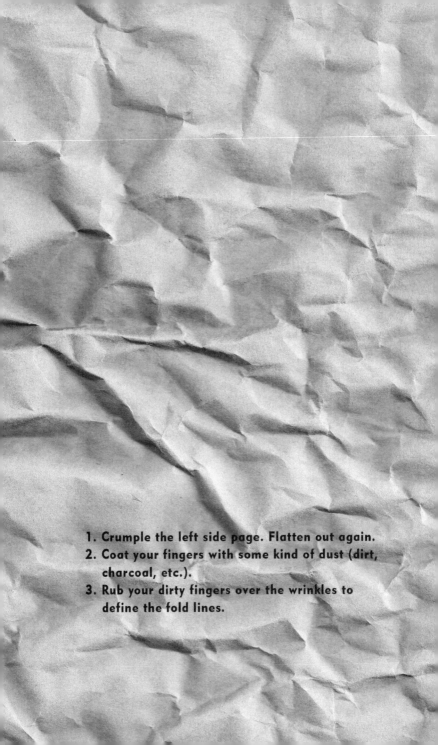

1. Crumple the left side page. Flatten out again.
2. Coat your fingers with some kind of dust (dirt, charcoal, etc.).
3. Rub your dirty fingers over the wrinkles to define the fold lines.

1. Do a painting in a water-based medium (pen, marker, watercolor, etc.).
2. Leave it out during a rain or snowstorm.

1. Alter this image by damaging it.
2. Find an interesting way to repair the damage.

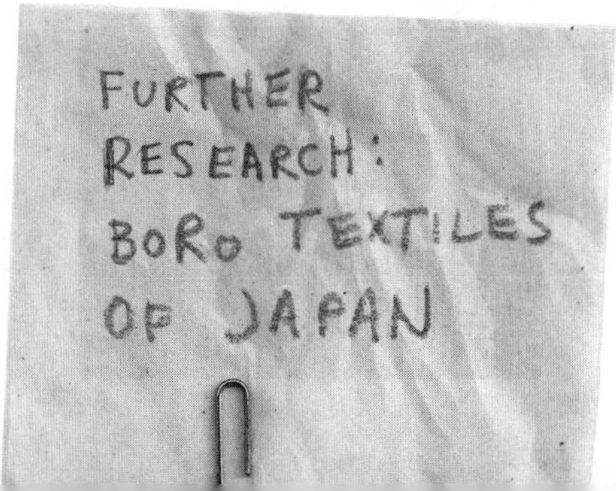
FURTHER
RESEARCH:
BORO TEXTILES
OF JAPAN

Re-create these lines.

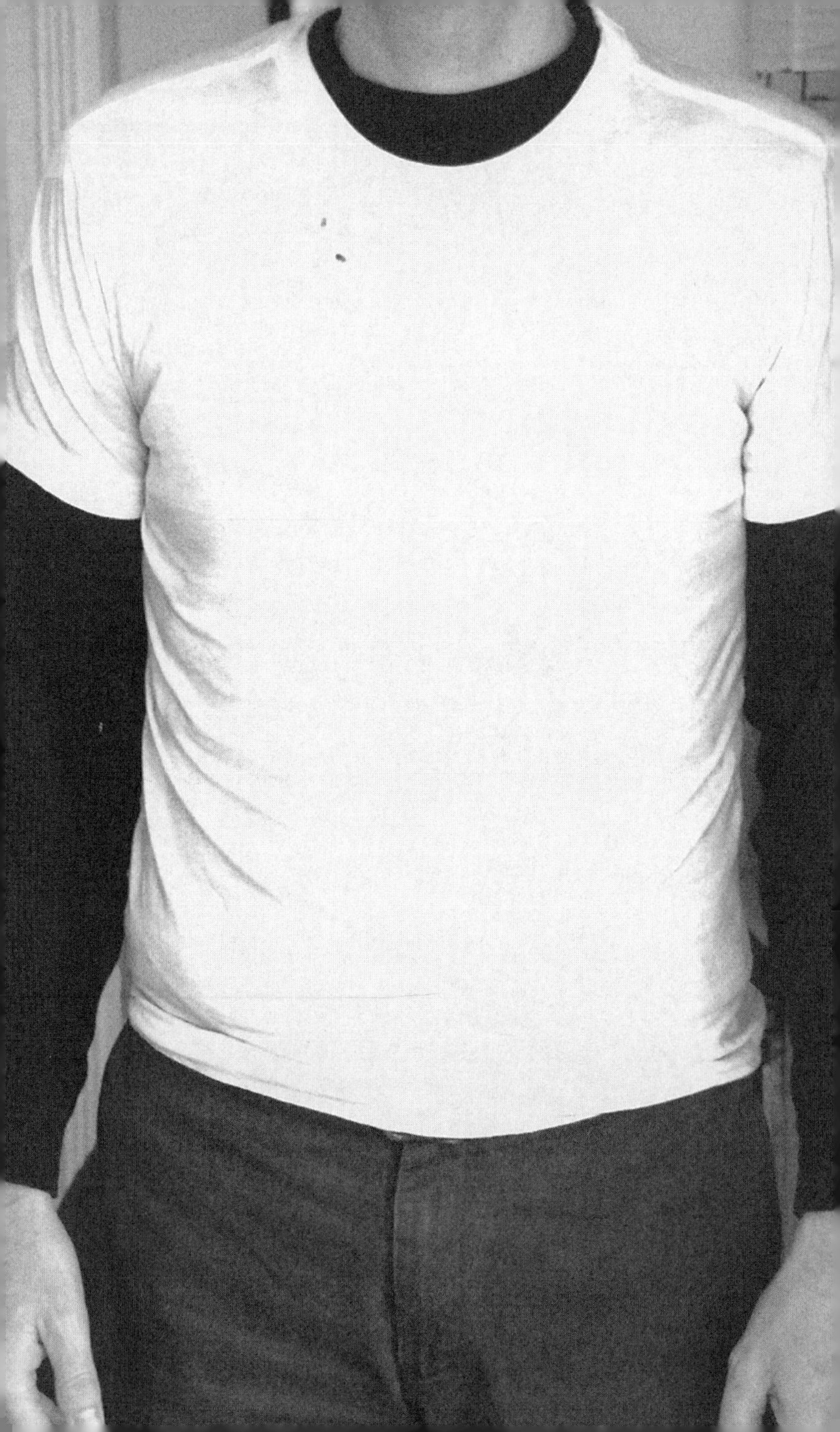

Mess up this shirt.
Some ideas: Crack an egg, wipe it off.
Splatter something. Drip ink. Doodle.

FURTHER RESEARCH:
JACKSON POLLOCK

Splatter, drip, and fling.

1. **Spill something onto your hand or face (ice cream, glue, etc.).**
2. **Use this space to remove the excess.**

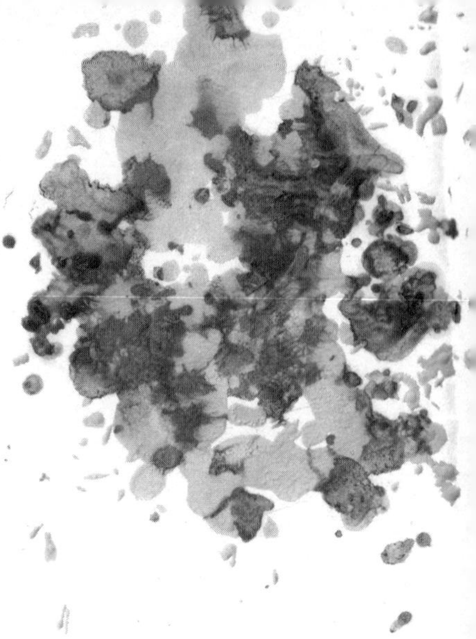

1. Take a couple of crayons.
2. Scrape the crayons with a knife to create shavings. Place shavings in middle of the left-hand page.
3. Fold the page in half.
4. Using an iron on a low setting, go over the folded page with a few quick passes until the wax melts.
5. Open page to reveal design.

1. Cut a shape out of cardboard to use as a stencil.
2. Drop the shape onto the page.
3. Paint or color around the shape.
4. Repeat.

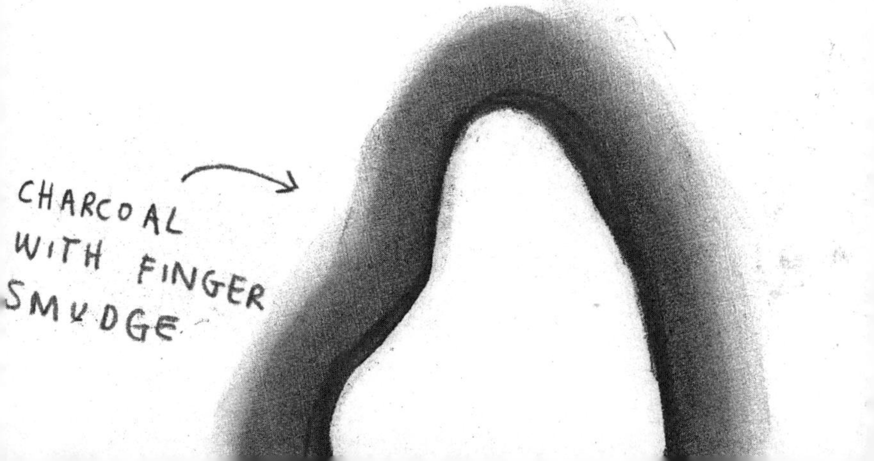

DISASTER AREA

This is a disaster area. Fill every square inch of this page with stuff.

For an entire day do all of your necessary tasks using your "wrong" hand. Record your exploits here (using your "wrong" hand).

Make a mess quickly without thinking. In one minute you must do ten different things to this page (i.e., break, stretch, tear, crush, fold). Ready. GO!

Add some harsh weather to this page (fog, snow, rain, etc.).

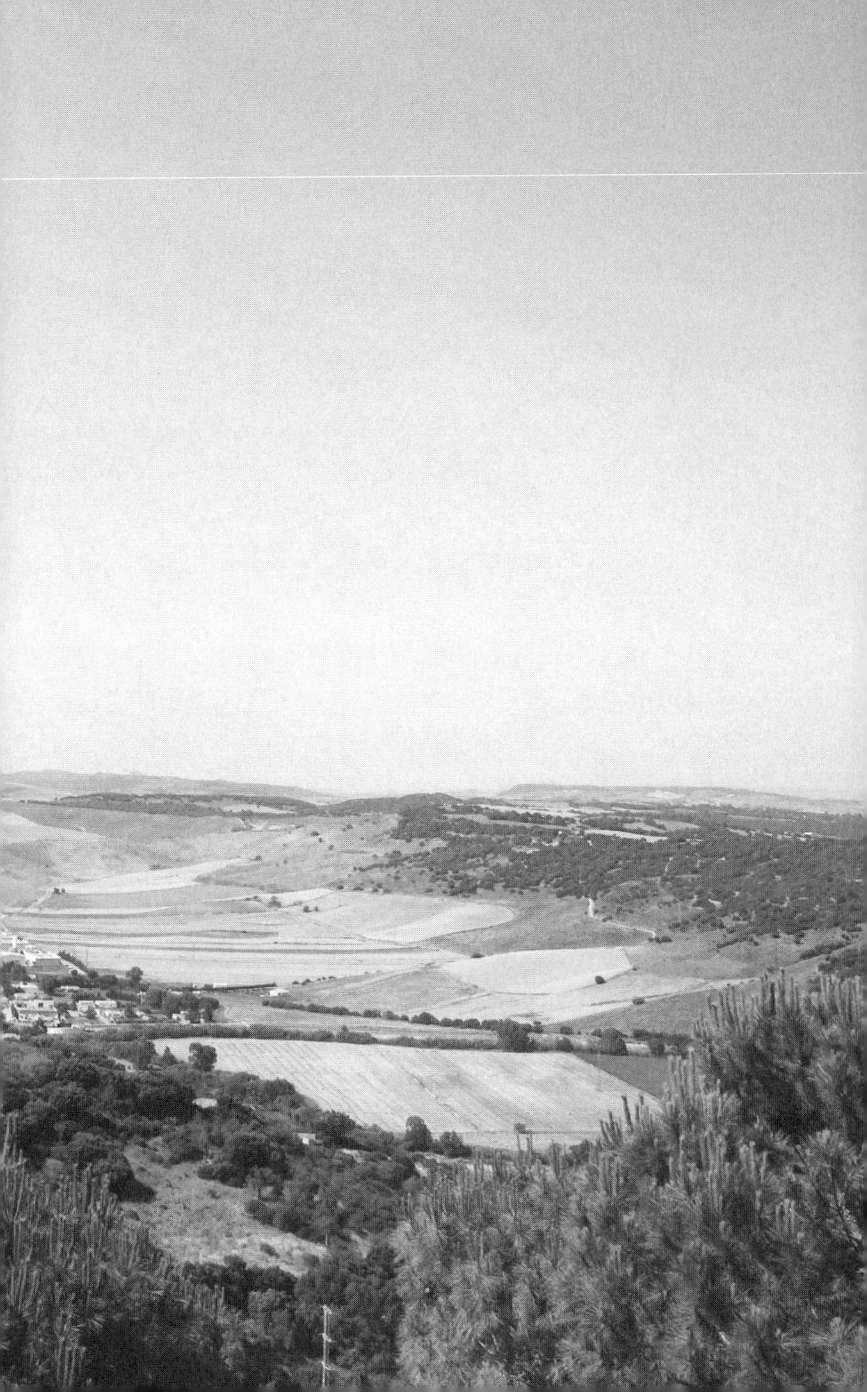

1. Soak this page with water.
2. Try to write on it.
Alternate: Drop ink onto wet page.

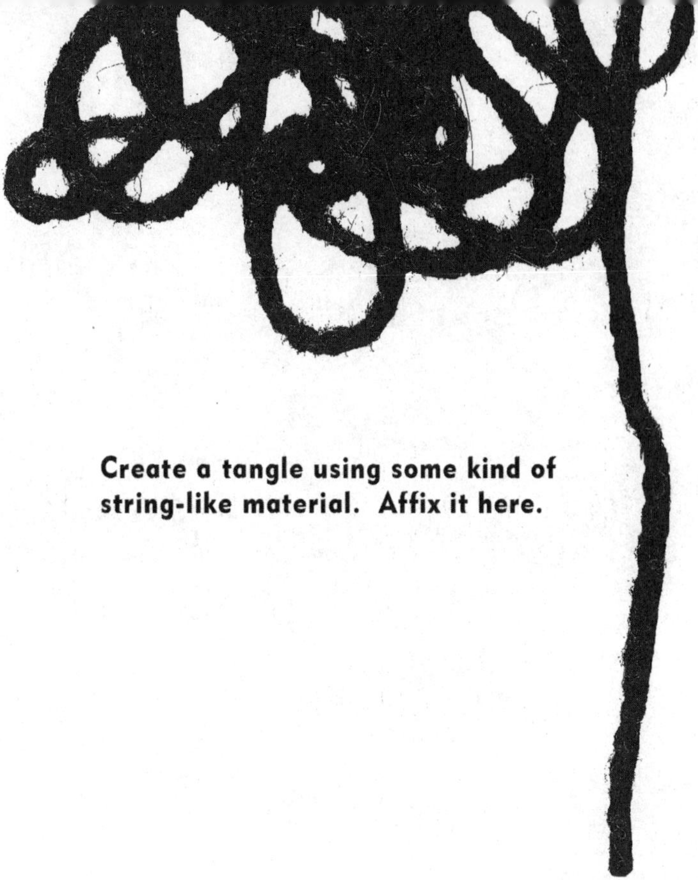

Create a tangle using some kind of string-like material. Affix it here.

Take an existing mess (spill, etc.) and find a way to amplify it. Make it bigger. Exaggerate it.

PERFECT

Alter this image by using a variety of techniques (e.g., scrubbing, tearing, sanding, etc.).

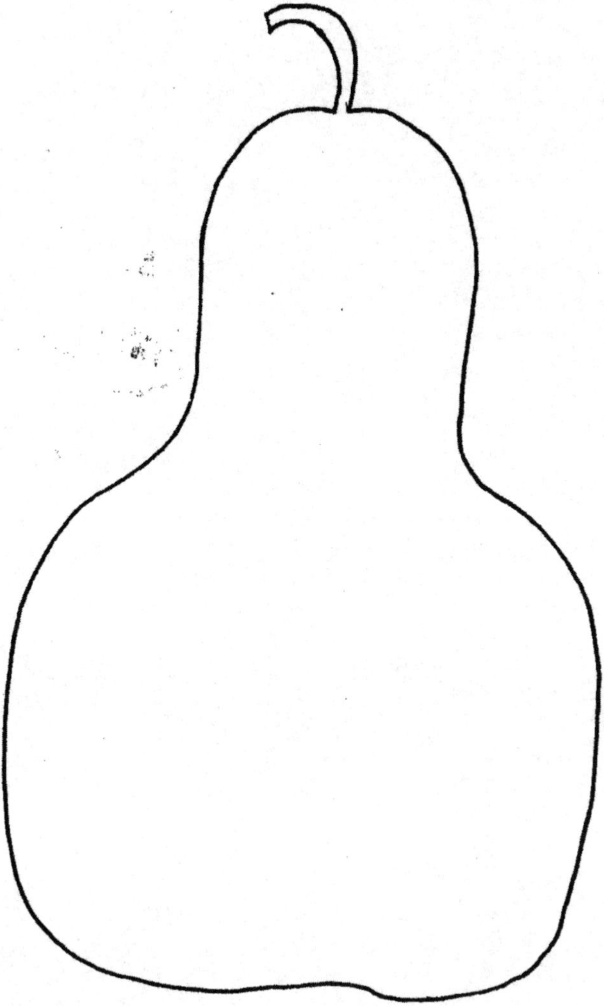

Color this in with your eyes closed (or in the dark).

1. **Bury this book.**
2. **After three days, dig it up.**

Try these various smudging techniques. With a wet medium (paint): drag an object over it (squeegee-like), blot with another piece of paper, drip water over top, blow. With a dry medium (pencil): rub with your finger, use some kind of solvent (water, alcohol), drag along the ground. Experiment with as many different materials as you can.

← 1. Do a drawing or painting here.
2. After seven days, destroy it.

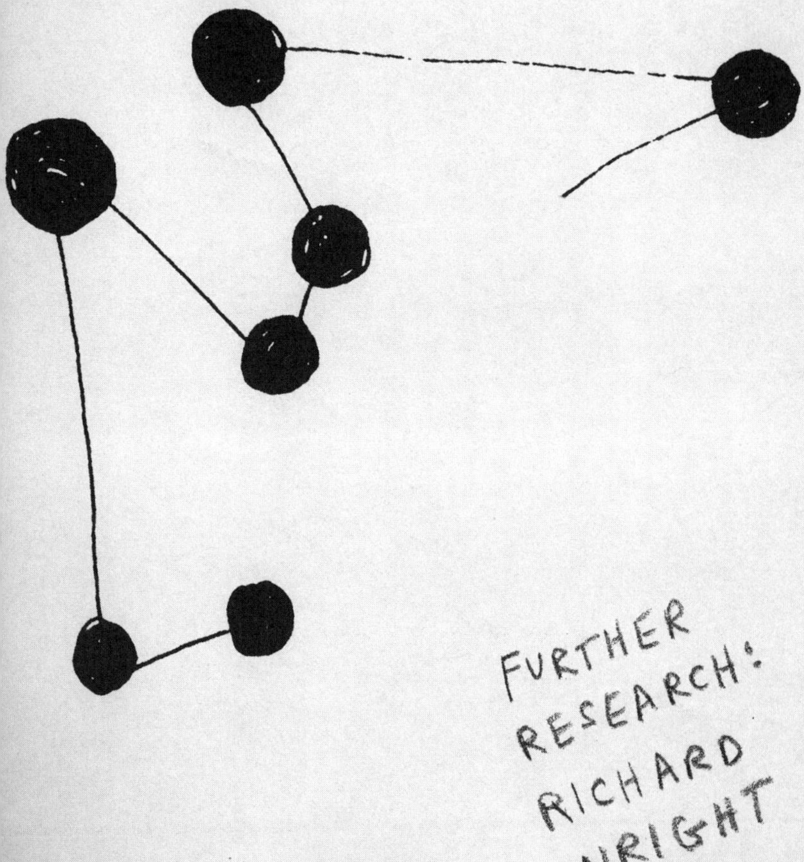
FURTHER
RESEARCH:
RICHARD
WRIGHT

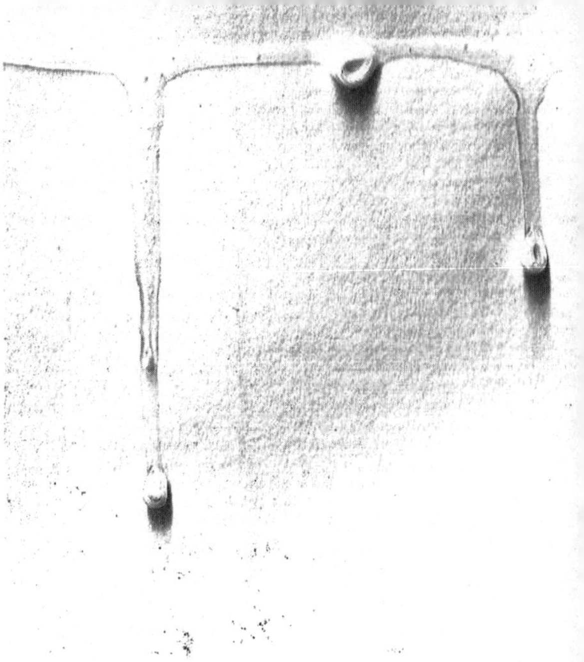

1. Apply a horizontal line of white glue to the top of this page.
2. Support the book somehow so the paint runs down the page as it dries.
3. Once it is dry, add a coat of ink or paint overtop. Let dry.
4. Sand the page slightly to bring out the glue shapes.

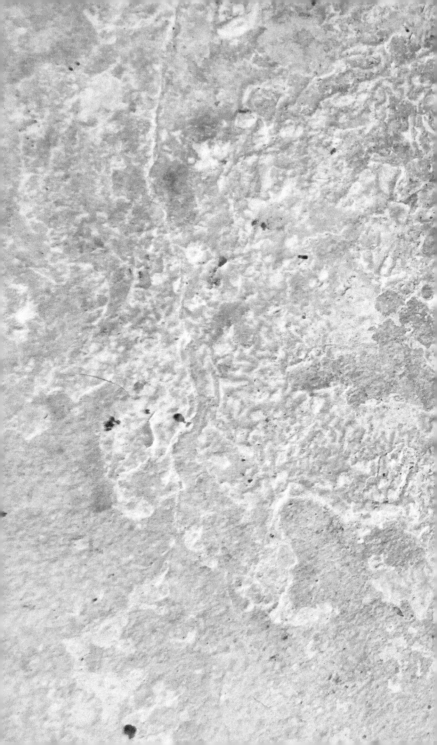

1. Get a hammer.
2. Take a drawing device such as a piece of chalk, charcoal, crayon, pencil, etc.
3. Smash.
4. Repeat.

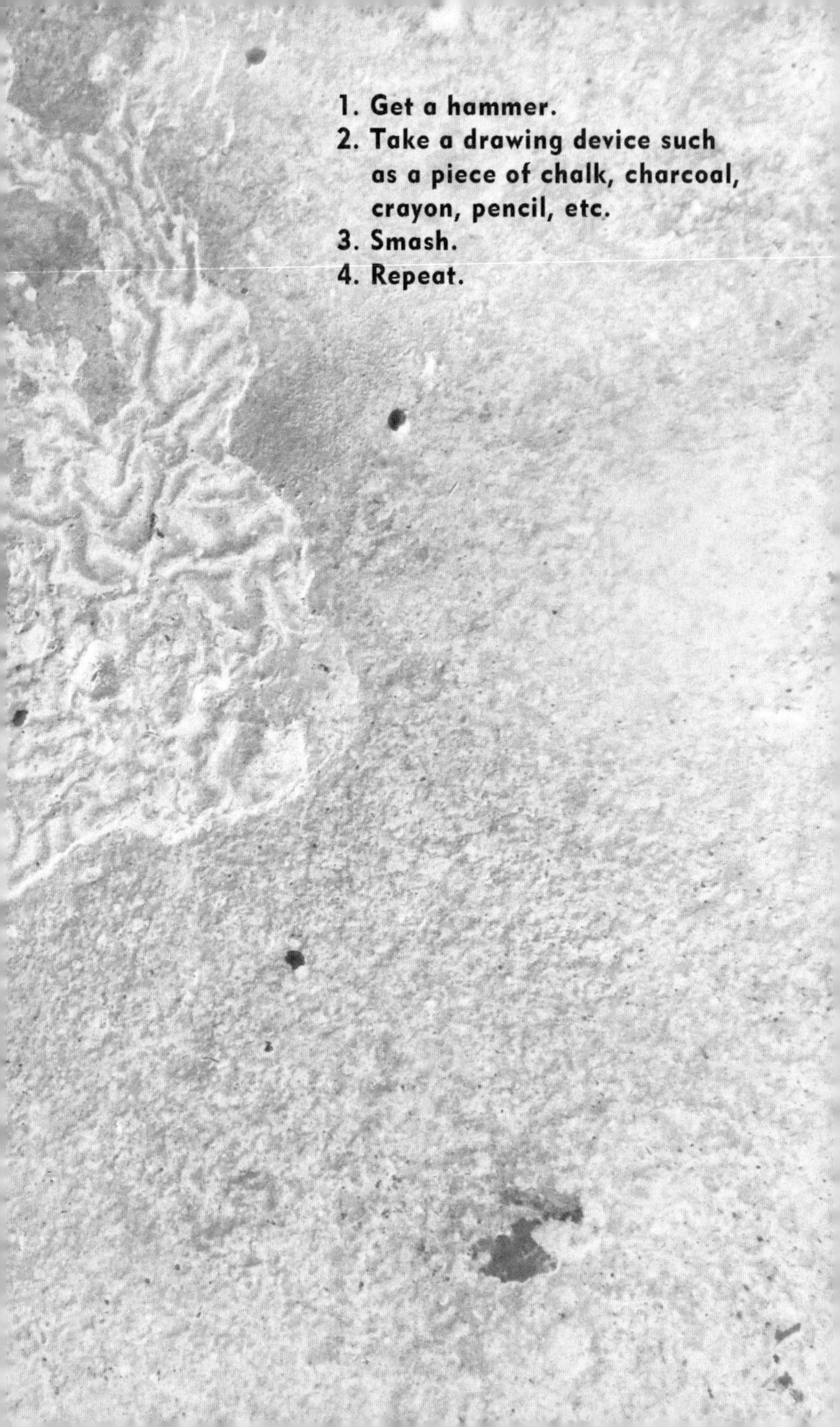

1. Find a long stick.
2. Tape a pen to the end of it.
3. Try to draw something holding the far end of the stick.

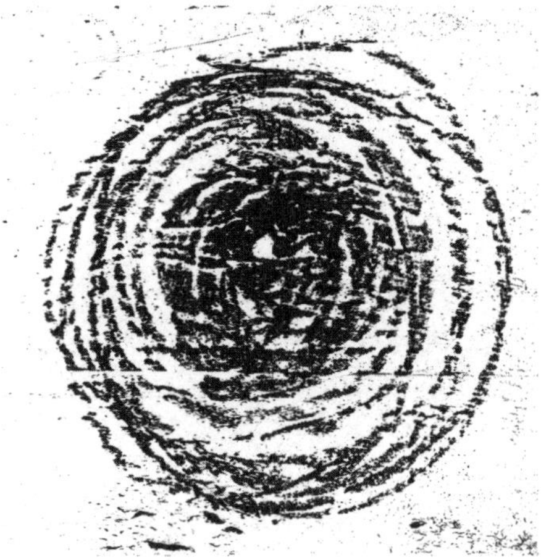

Draw the sun using ten different methods.

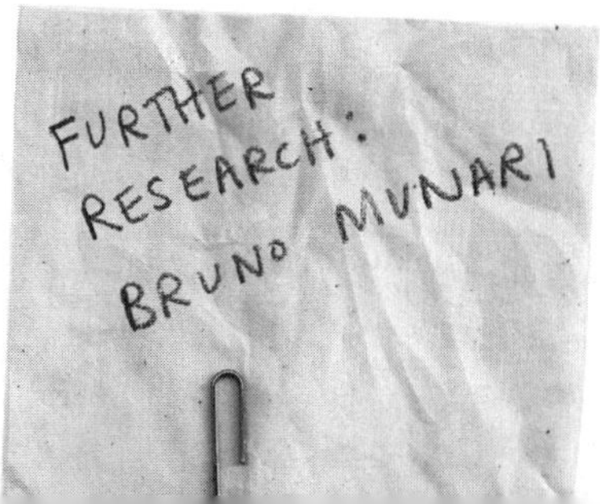
FURTHER
RESEARCH:
BRUNO MUNARI

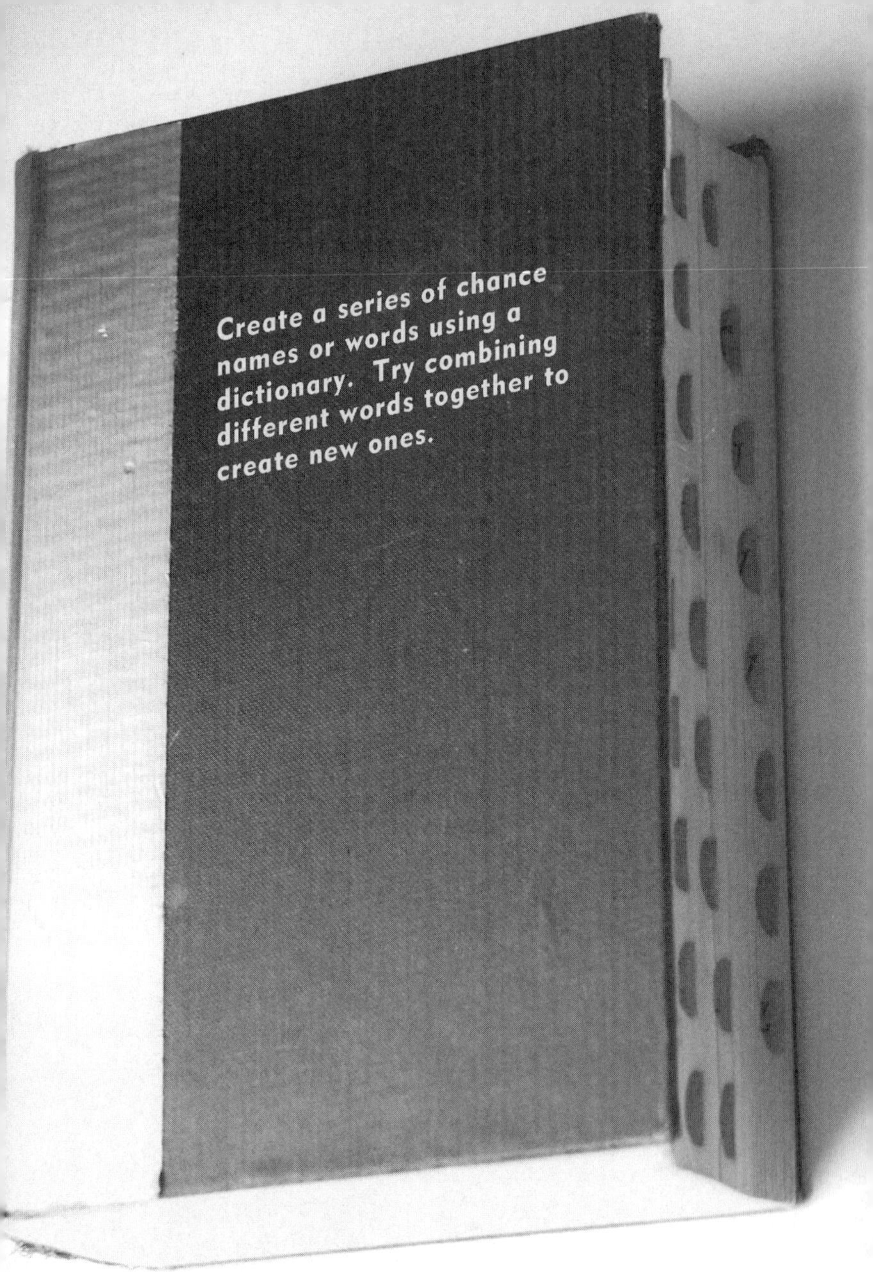
Create a series of chance names or words using a dictionary. Try combining different words together to create new ones.

FURTHER RESEARCH: ALAN FLETCHER

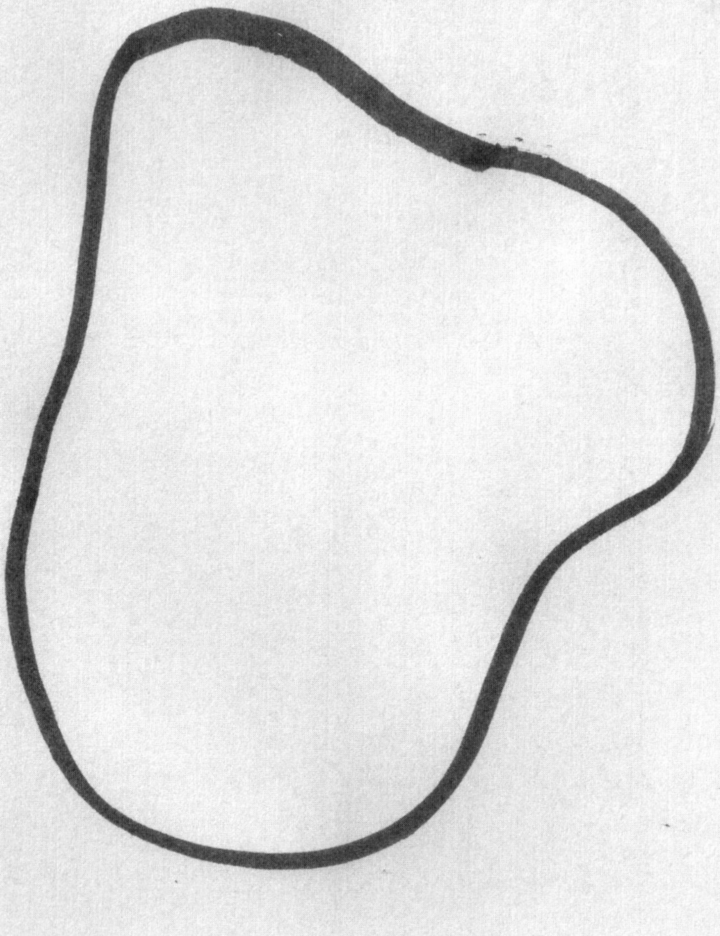

Trace this line as fast as you can for several minutes.

PUBLIC MESS

Create a small mess out in public. Leave it for someone else to find. Encourage others to add to it. (Ideas: pile of stones, series of lines, a drawing, a footprint, etc.)

1. Drop an amount of ink onto a page to create a random blob.
2. Create a character out of it.
3. Repeat.

This man looks like he needs to let loose a little. You might want to help him out. A new hat, some glasses, facial hair perhaps?

Continue this picture.

SOMETIMES IT IS GOOD TO PLAY WITH YOUR FOOD.

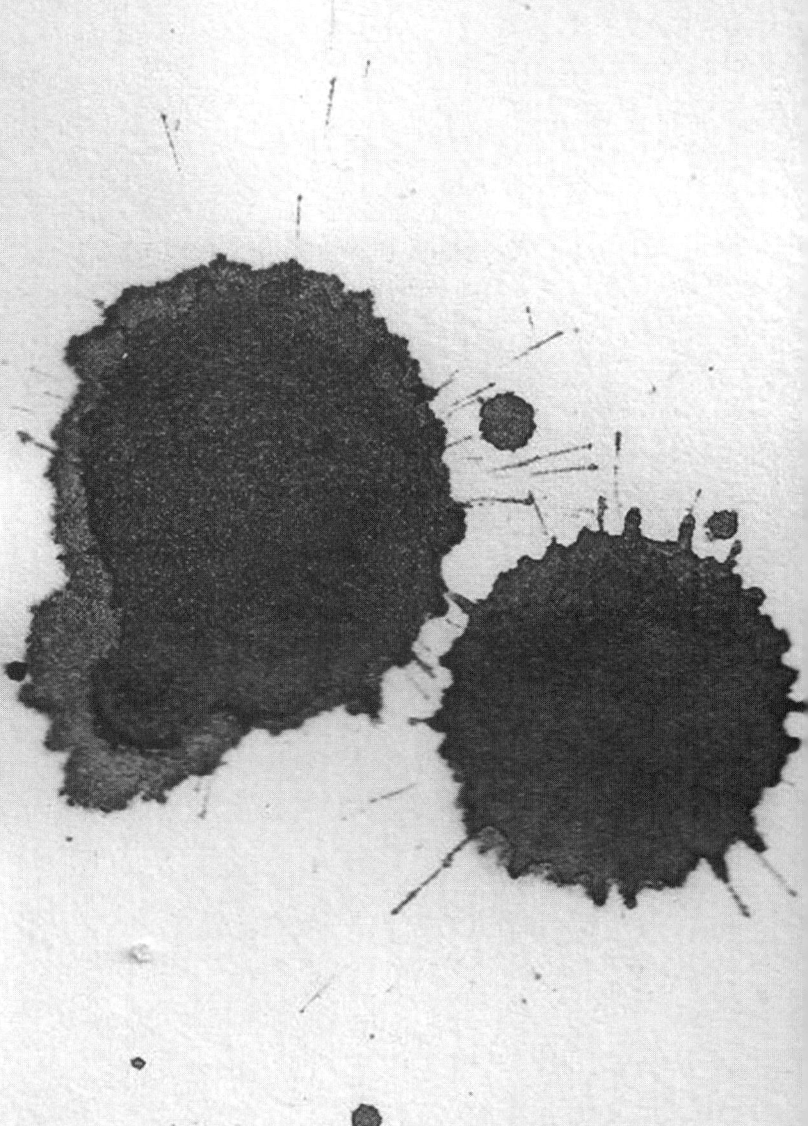

Abrasion test. Sand this image until it is gone.

FURTHER RESEARCH: FLUXUS

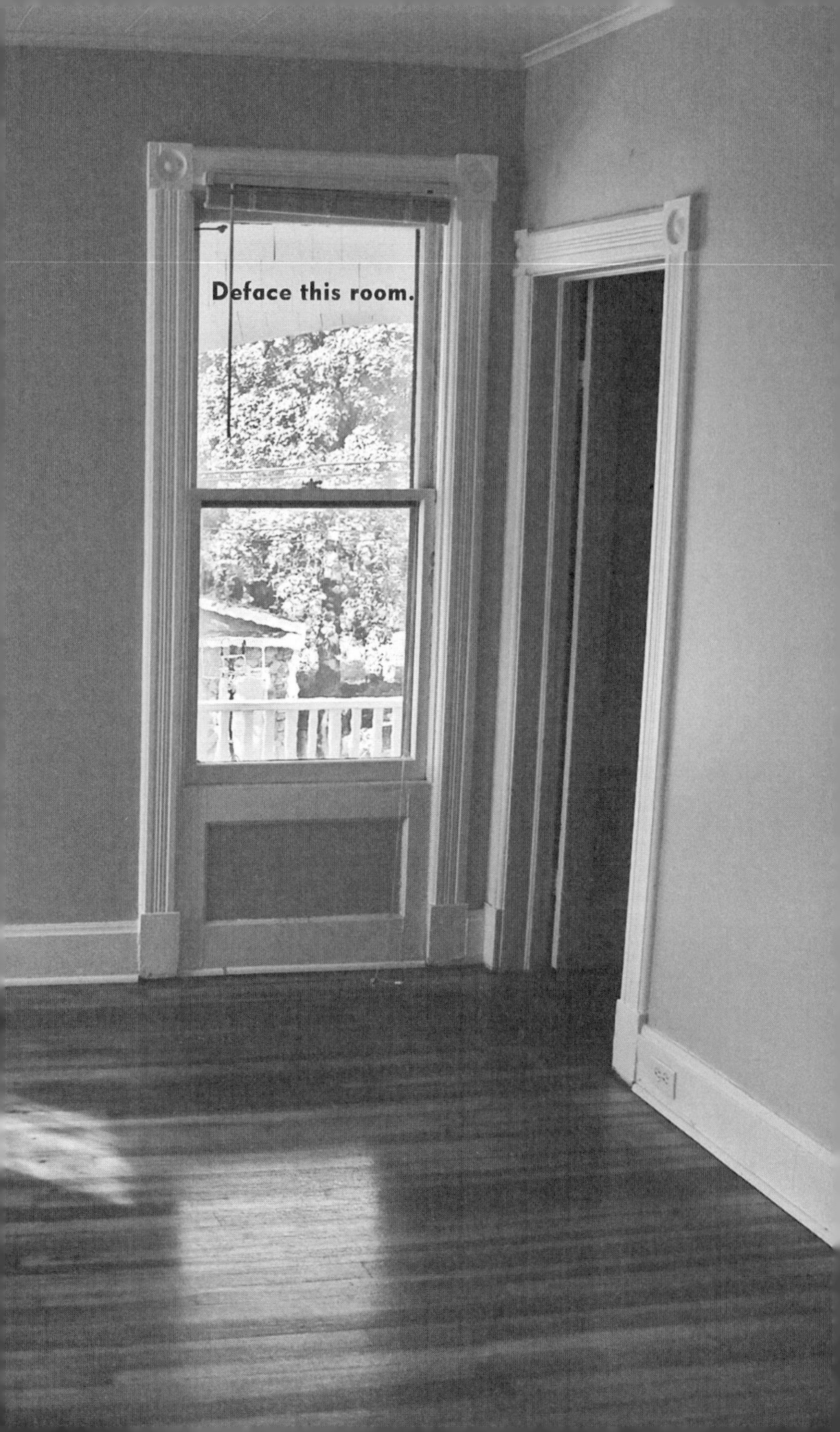
Deface this room.

Create a series of thumbprints as the basis for drawing other objects (i.e., doodle over top of them). Also try working with handprints.

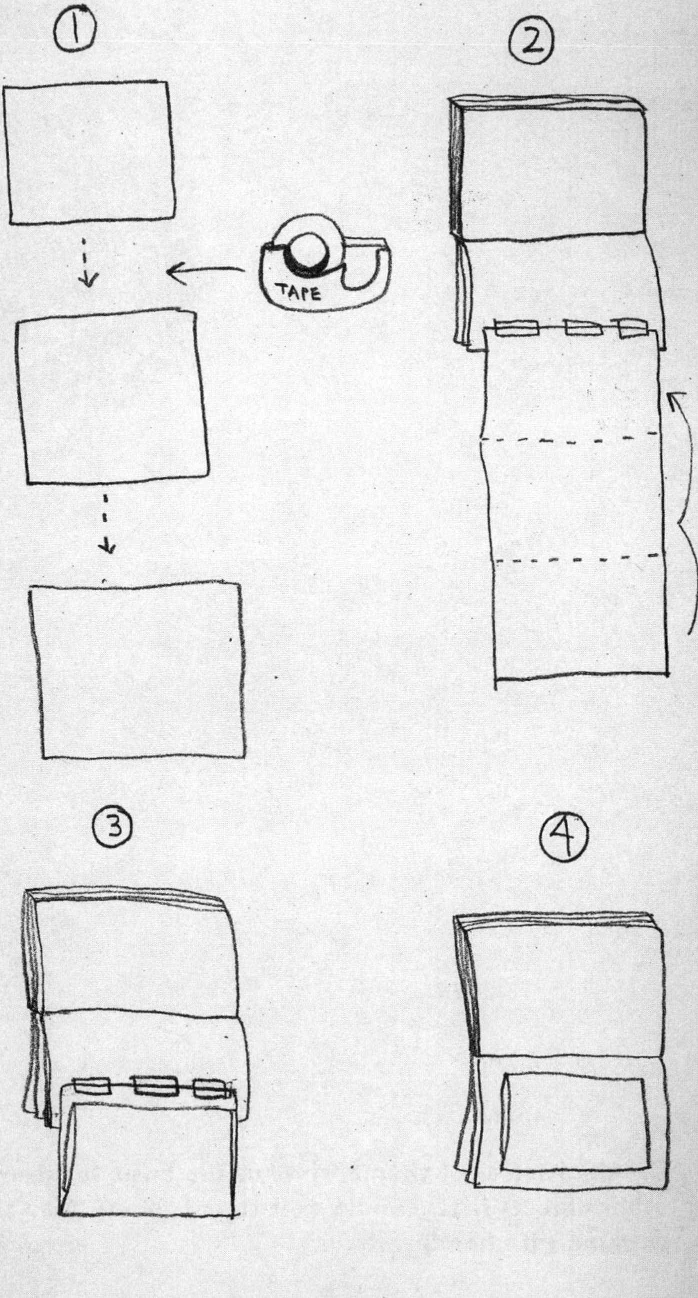
1
TAPE
2
3
4

1. **Create an extra-long page by taping a few extra sheets of paper to this page.**
2. **Create a spill (so that it looks like it is spilling out onto the floor).**

1. Scratch on the black page (create a series of different textures).
2. Cut out some shapes.
3. Make a five-minute collage.

1. **Find a magazine.**
2. **Turn to page 32.**
3. **If there is a photo on that page cut it out. (If there is no photo, try page 50.)**
4. **Make connections between yourself and the image in as many ways as possible.**

Alternate: Acquire a photo of someone else's family.

ON A JOURNEY
NO MATTER WHERE.
—HERMANN HESSE

FIELD TRIP

1. Go on an adventure with no money.
2. Document it here.

RECIPE:

AMOUNT	INGREDIENTS	DIRECTIONS

Create your own recipe using only things you have in your fridge and cupboards. Attempt something you've never made before.

1. Start with a simple drawing (a shape, a word, a line).
2. Every day for one month add something to the page. Experiment with many different mediums and techniques. You can also experiment with erasing parts as well.
3. Document the process with photos. (If you wish you can put all the photos together to make a stop motion animation.)

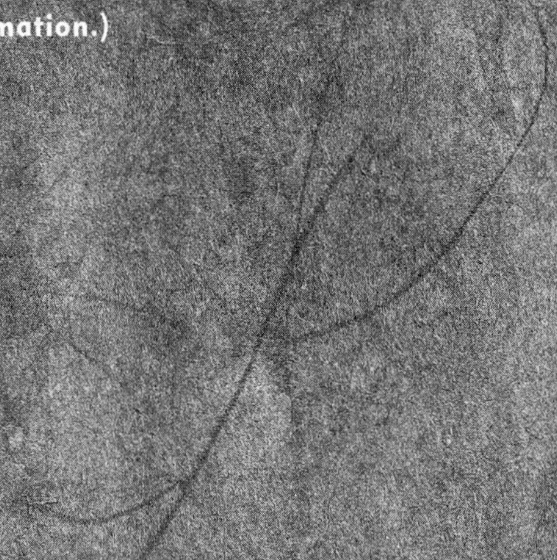

FURTHER RESEARCH : JENNI ROPE

Fill in this five-inch square by using all of the colors you have on hand.

FURTHER RESEARCH: SOL LEWITT

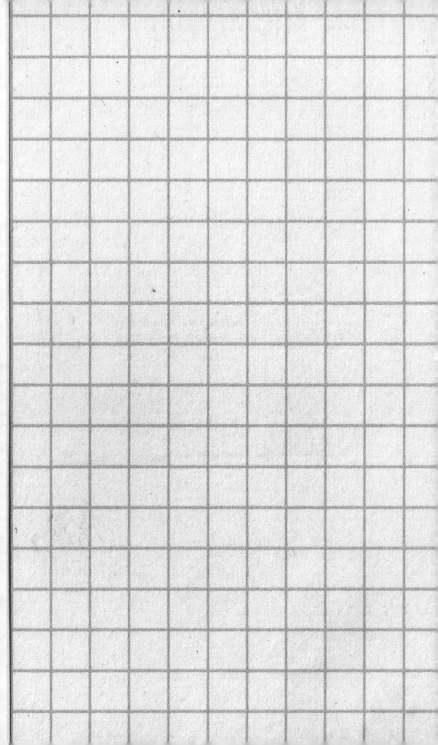

1. Select a series of ten colors in any medium.
2. Fill in each square in this grid in some kind of regular sequence.
3. Insert a mistake somewhere.

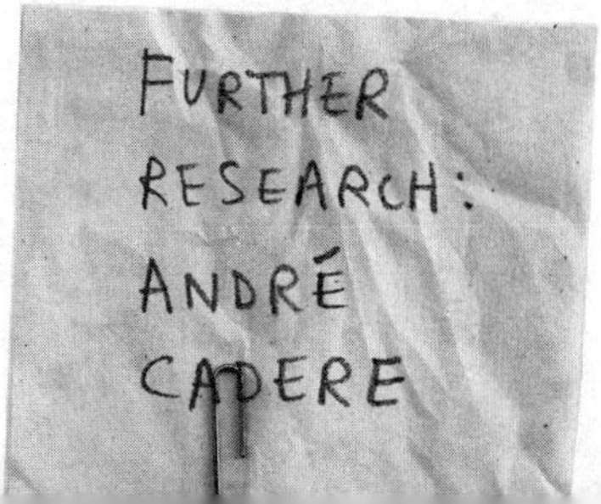
FURTHER
RESEARCH:
ANDRÉ
CADERE

1. Use this page to sweep up dirt in your room.
2. Find a way to contain the dirt here.
3. Use the dirt in an art piece.

EVERYBODY IS
BORN AN
INVENTOR.

—R. BUCKMINSTER
FULLER

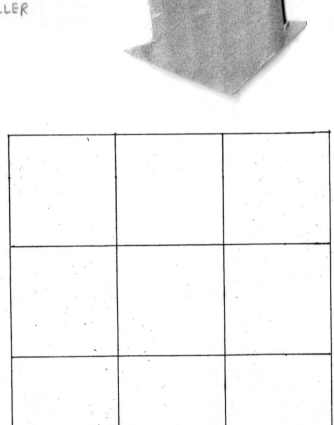

FURTHER
RESEARCH:
EVA HESSE

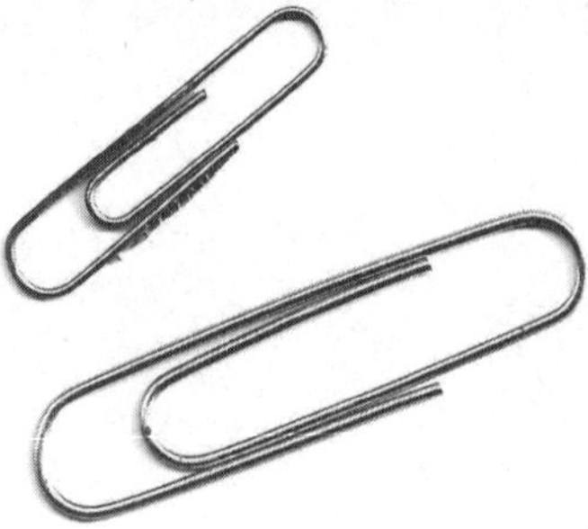

RANDOM SCULPTURE

1. On each of the squares write the name of an everyday object you have on hand. (Some ideas: paper, cardboard, can, egg carton, toilet paper roll, paper clips, string, twigs, rocks, plastic bags, cereal box, fabric, etc.)
2. Cut out the squares and put them in a hat. Pick three.
3. Create a sculpture using only what you have chosen.
4. Document it with a photo.

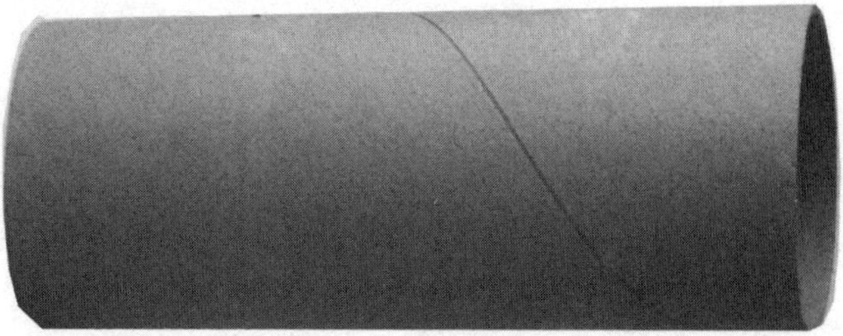

DÉTOURNEMENT

Alter this image, or deface it to change the meaning of it completely.

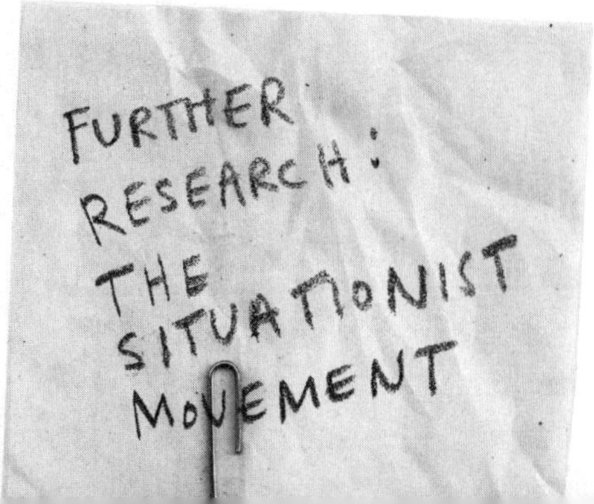
FURTHER
RESEARCH:
THE
SITUATIONIST
MOVEMENT

photo credit: Ignoto

Fill this tree with interesting things.

DRAWING TO SOUNDS

In this exercise the sounds in your environment determine what you draw. (Works best if you are in a sound-intensive environment.) If you are hearing many sounds at once you must pick one to draw to.

high-pitched sounds = circles
low-pitched sounds = straight lines
human voices = small dots
machine sounds = fast scribble
traffic sounds = lines that stop and start

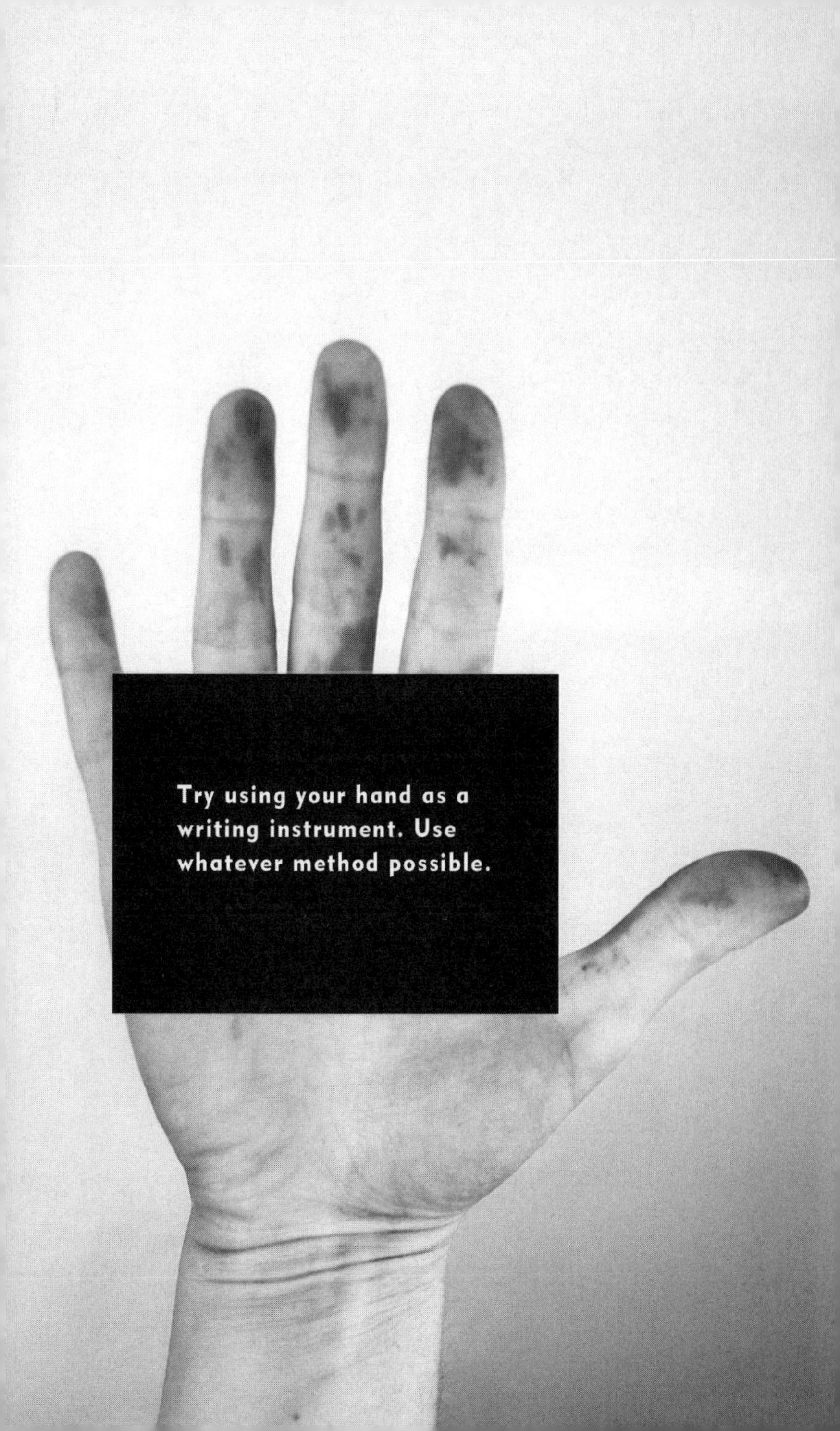
Try using your hand as a
writing instrument. Use
whatever method possible.

A page to stick only blue things.

SUBCONSCIOUS MESS

1. Set out a bunch of supplies (pencils, paints, etc.). Write or draw without censoring.
2. Make a move solely by using your intuition.

RESEARCH: AUTOMATIC WRITING OR DRAWING USED BY THE SURREALISTS

THERE'S NOTHING WE REALLY NEED TO DO THAT ISN'T DANGEROUS.

— JOHN CAGE

GROUP MESS

Start scribbling here (it has already been started for you). Ask some friends to help you finish the whole page.

Take a series of blurry photos on purpose.

WRITING MESS

1. Write a sentence on each line.
2. Cut out strips.
3. Recombine sentences to create new poems.

Alternate:

1. Take a paragraph from one of your favorite writers.
2. Copy it here.
3. Cut it up.
4. Rearrange the words.

FURTHER RESEARCH:
RAYMOND QUENEAU
AND OULIPO

Fill in this paint-by-number using random colors.

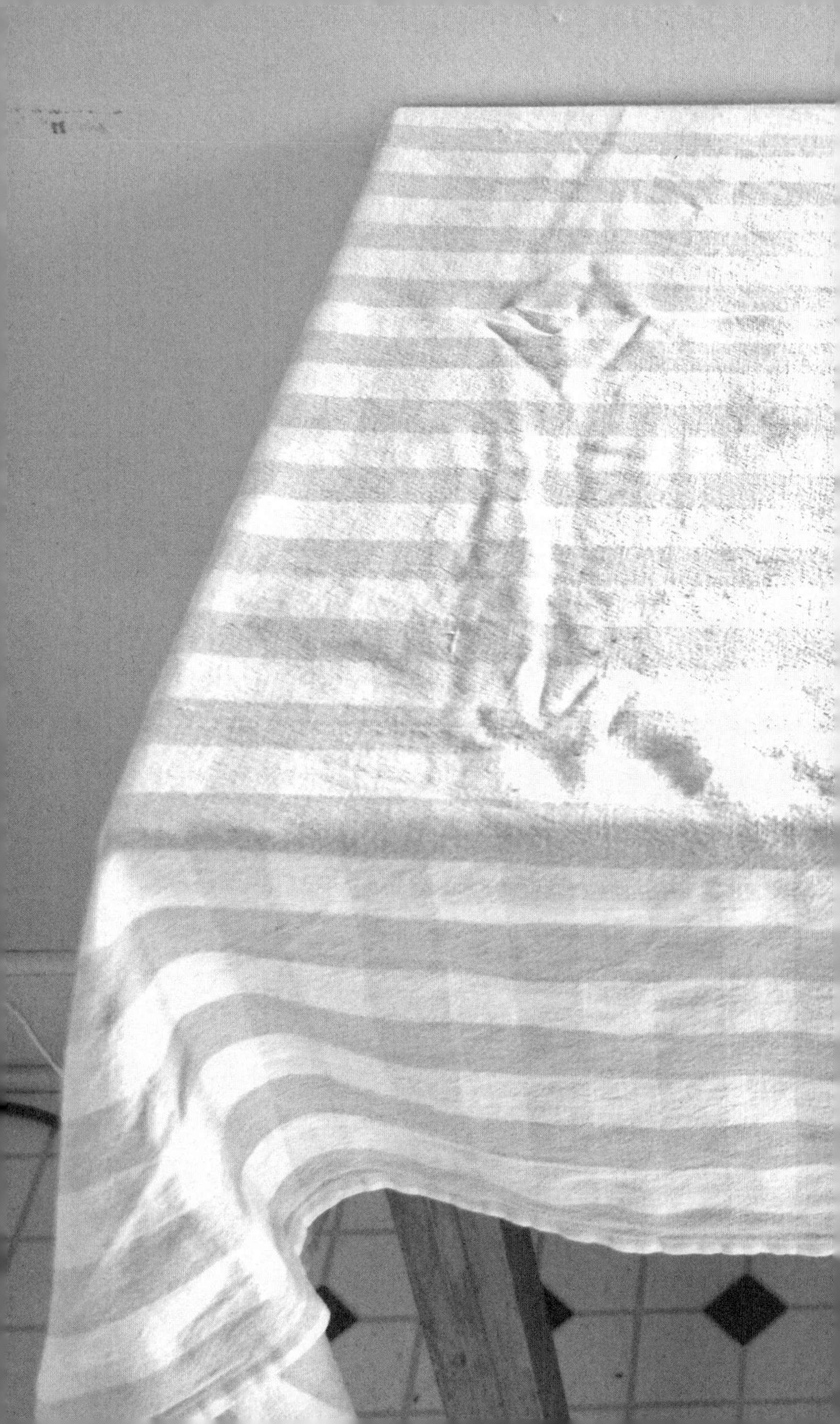

Create a mess here with a friend while having lunch together.

SHORT ATTENTION SPAN PAGE

Do something in each square for only 10 seconds.

Lose your balance. Do something that throws you off-kilter. Attempt to record it in some way (photo, video, writing).

FURTHER RESEARCH: BAS JAN ADER

1. Take a magazine or a newspaper.
2. Cut a shape out of several layers.
3. Arrange the shapes into some configuration to make a collage.
4. Glue them down.

Alternate: Cover page with glue and drop the shapes, letting them stay where they land.

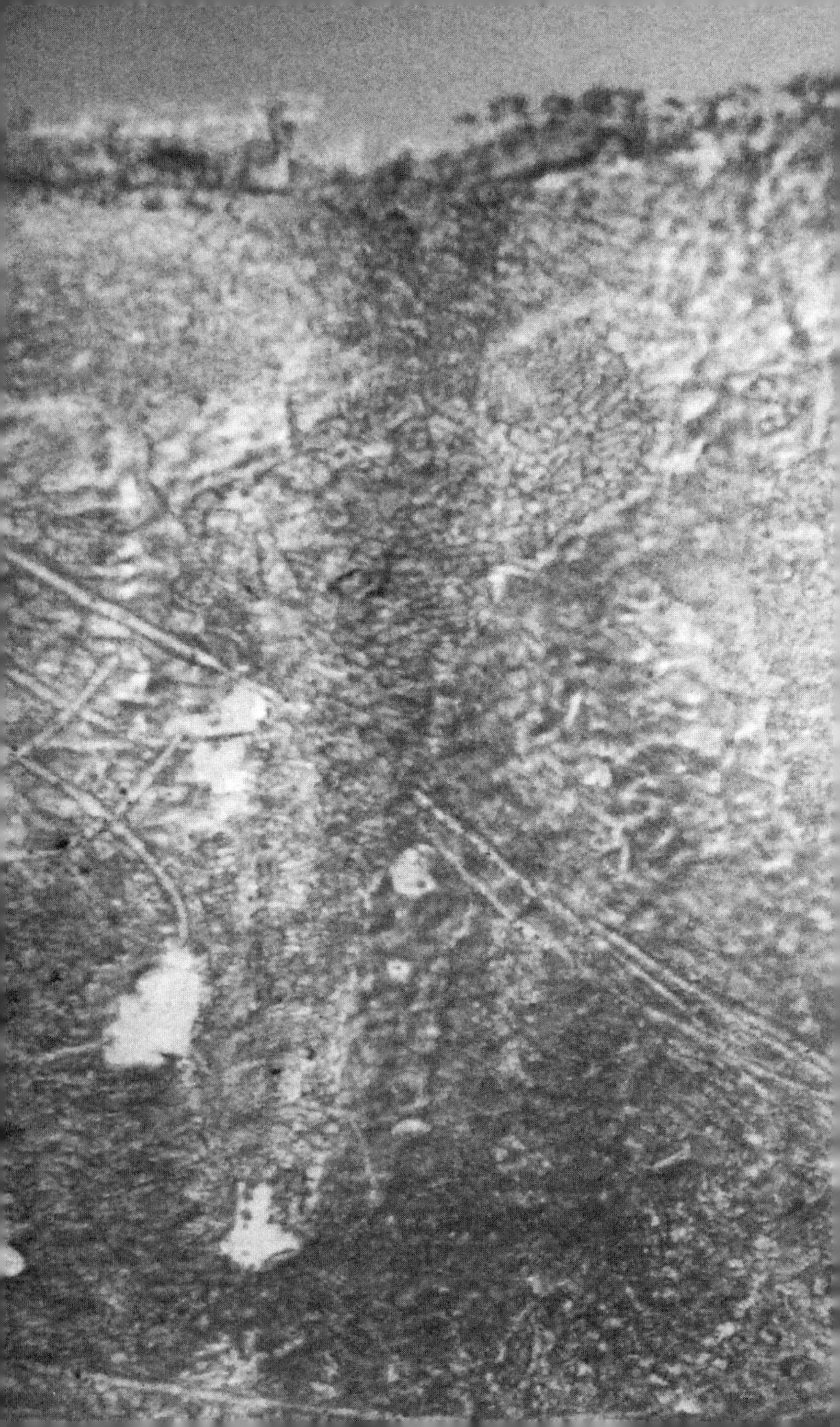

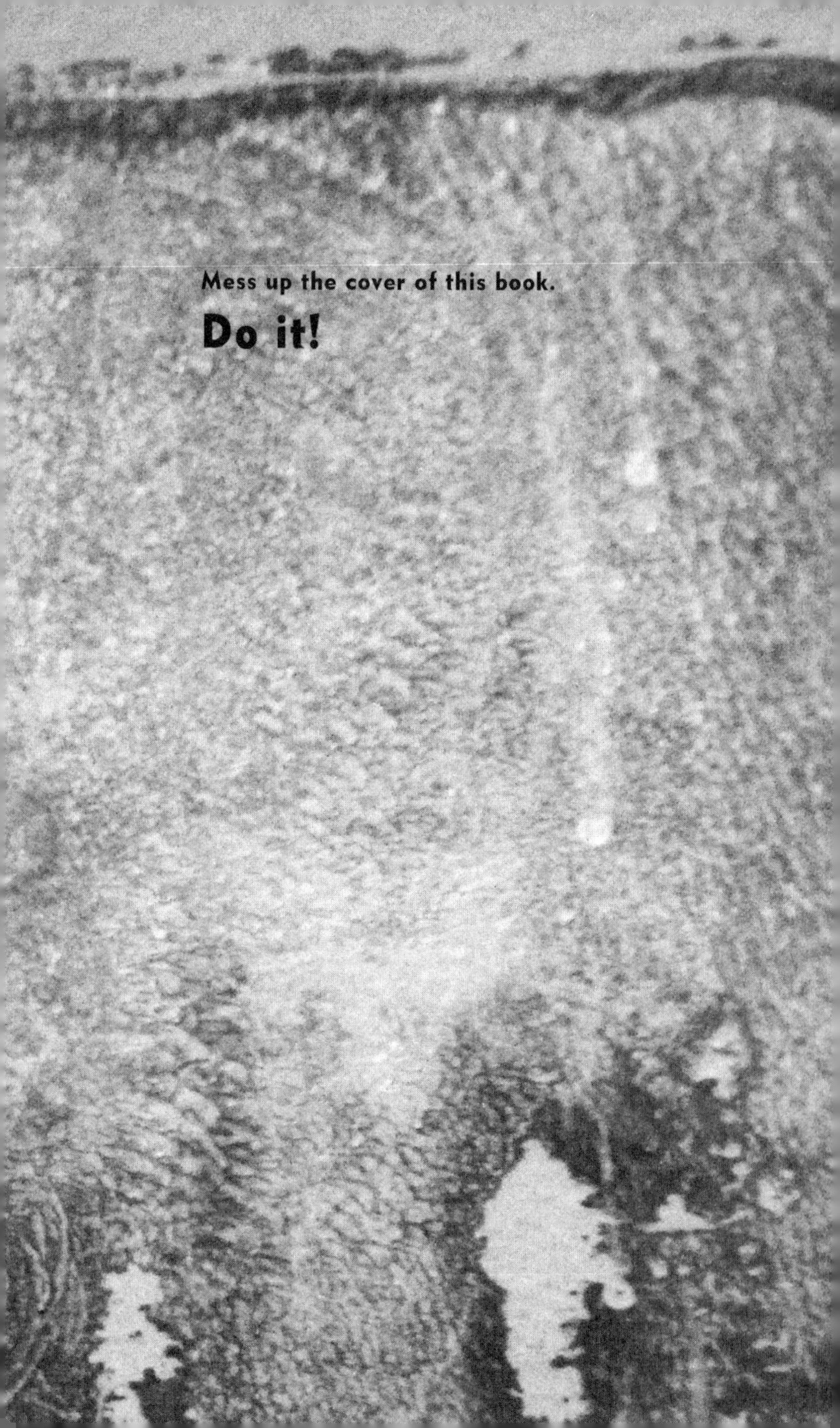

Mess up the cover of this book.

Do it!

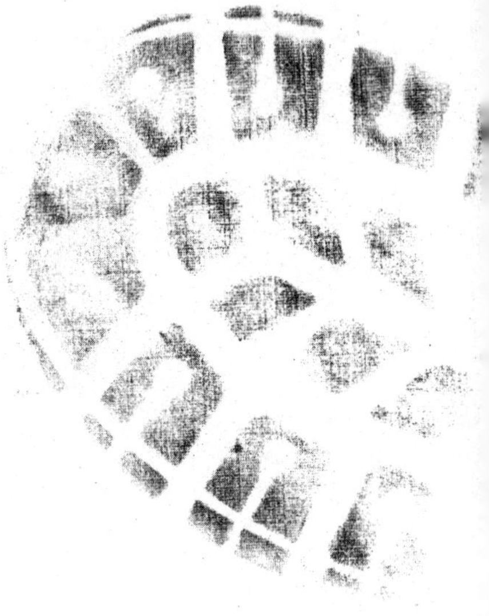

GROUP MESS

1. Create something here (a drawing, a word, a texture).
2. Ask a friend to add something to the page. (It's okay if it covers up your image.*)
3. Do something to alter what your friend did.
4. Repeat.

*Document the stages with photos if possible.

SMUDGE LOG

1. Create random smudges in each of these squares while you are going about your day. Experiment with different substances.
2. Document where and when each smudge was made.

DATE	DATE	DATE	DATE
TIME	TIME	TIME	TIME
LOCATION	LOCATION	LOCATION	LOCATION
DATE	DATE	DATE	DATE
TIME	TIME	TIME	TIME
LOCATION	LOCATION	LOCATION	LOCATION
DATE	DATE	DATE	DATE
TIME	TIME	TIME	TIME
LOCATION	LOCATION	LOCATION	LOCATION
DATE	DATE	DATE	DATE
TIME	TIME	TIME	TIME
LOCATION	LOCATION	LOCATION	LOCATION

photo credit: Arthur Dietrich, Seebad Heringsdorf u. Ostseebad Koserow

Delete or erase something.

1. Spill a substance here (some things that work well are coffee, tea, etc.). Let it dry.
2. Look for shapes in the dried substance, draw things based on what shapes you find (faces, characters, etc.).

1. Coat this page with paint.
2. Crumple up a piece of ordinary paper.
3. Drag the crumpled paper over the wet surface.

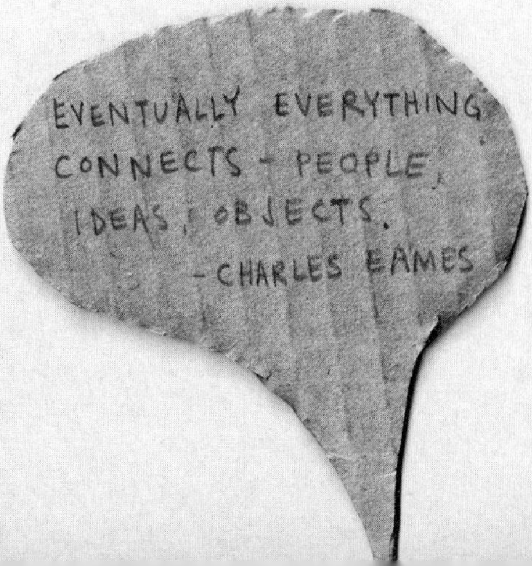
EVENTUALLY EVERYTHING
CONNECTS - PEOPLE,
IDEAS, OBJECTS.
-CHARLES EAMES

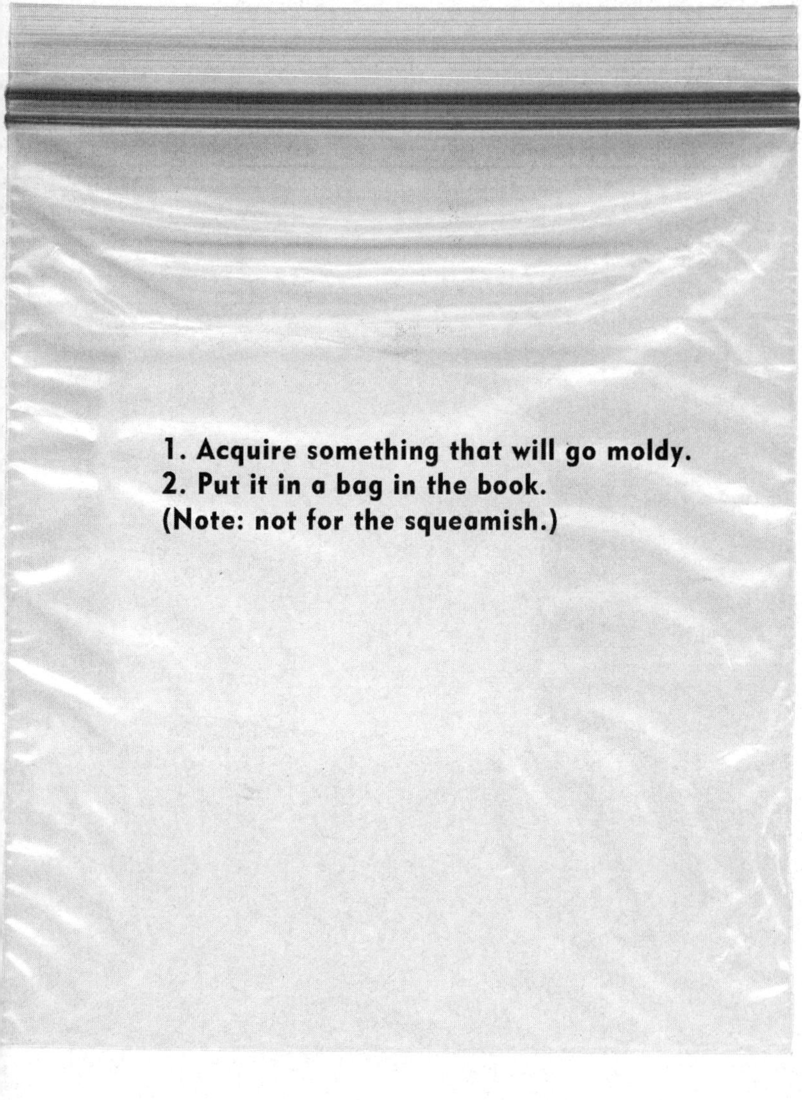

1. Acquire something that will go moldy.
2. Put it in a bag in the book.
(Note: not for the squeamish.)

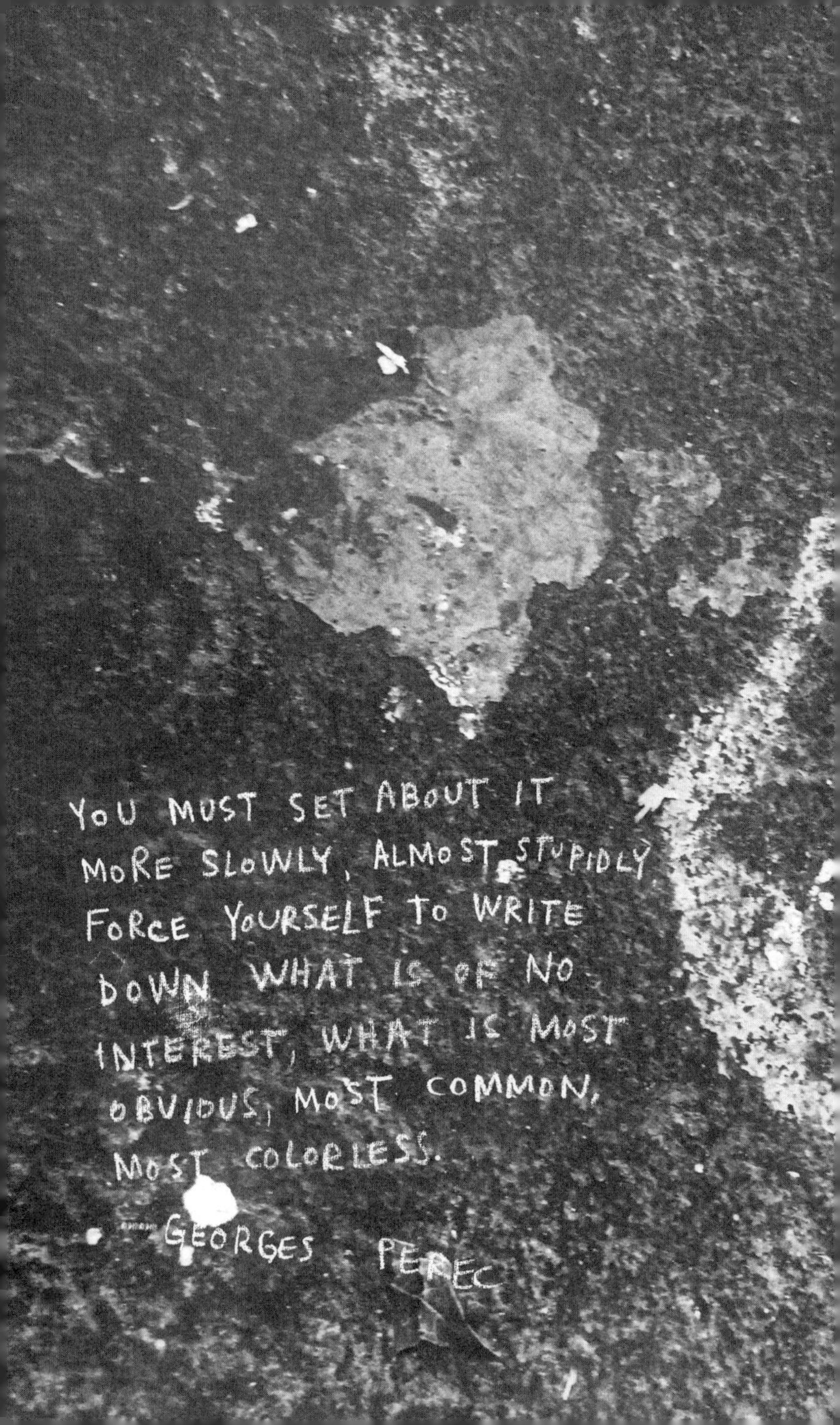
YOU MUST SET ABOUT IT
MORE SLOWLY, ALMOST STUPIDLY
FORCE YOURSELF TO WRITE
DOWN WHAT IS OF NO
INTEREST, WHAT IS MOST
OBVIOUS, MOST COMMON,
MOST COLORLESS.
— GEORGES PEREC

FIELD TRIP: DOCUMENTATION

1. Go out into the world.
2. Find examples of various messes, spills, drips, accidents, grafitti.
3. Document them in some way.

Use this page as a palette. Mix colors, test brushstrokes, etc.

FURTHER RESEARCH:

CHINESE CALLIGRAPHY

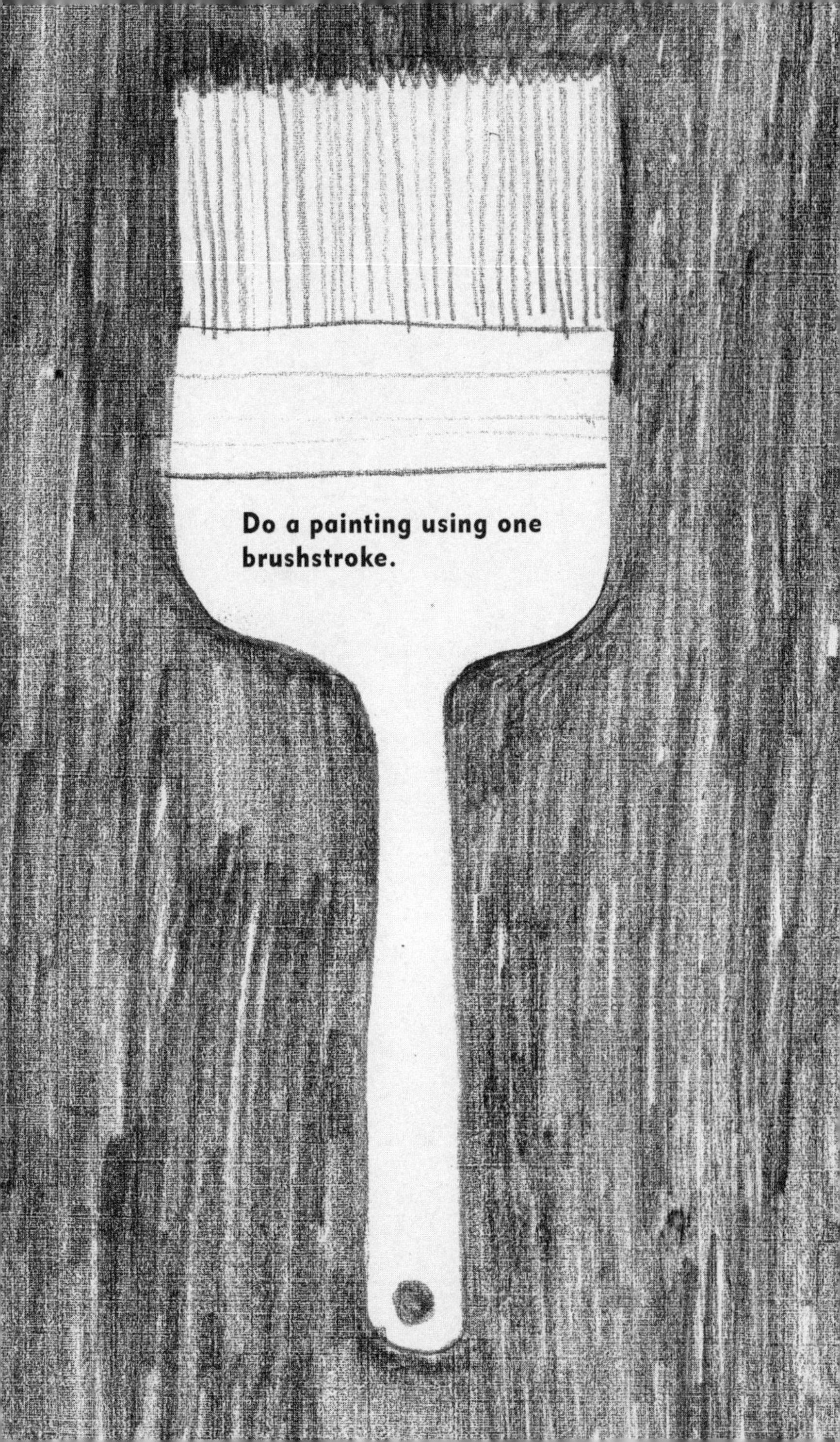
Do a painting using one brushstroke.

BLIND PHOTOGRAPHS

1. Point your camera without looking in the viewfinder.
2. Repeat. Take at least a dozen photos this way.

SCRIBBLE LOG

1. Create random scribbles in each of these squares while you are going about your day. Experiment with different utensils.
2. Document where and when each scribble was made.

DATE	DATE	DATE	DATE
TIME	TIME	TIME	TIME
LOCATION	LOCATION	LOCATION	LOCATION
DATE	DATE	DATE	DATE
TIME	TIME	TIME	TIME
LOCATION	LOCATION	LOCATION	LOCATION
DATE	DATE	DATE	DATE
TIME	TIME	TIME	TIME
LOCATION	LOCATION	LOCATION	LOCATION
DATE	DATE	DATE	DATE
TIME	TIME	TIME	TIME
LOCATION	LOCATION	LOCATION	LOCATION

Smear something here with your hands
purely for the tactile sensation.

DAILY MESSES

–take a picture of your bed every morning when you get out of it
–take a picture of your bedhead
–take a picture of your breakfast remnants

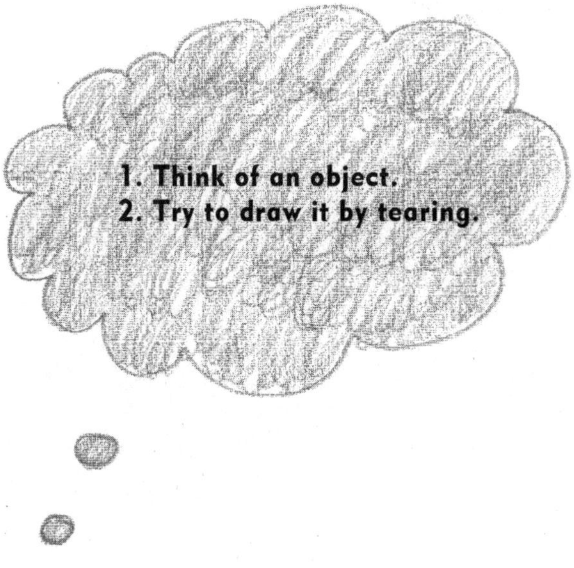
1. Think of an object.
2. Try to draw it by tearing.

Fill this page with things you can crumble.

1. **Take the image to the right and cut it into pieces.**
2. **Rearrange the image to create a new image entirely.**

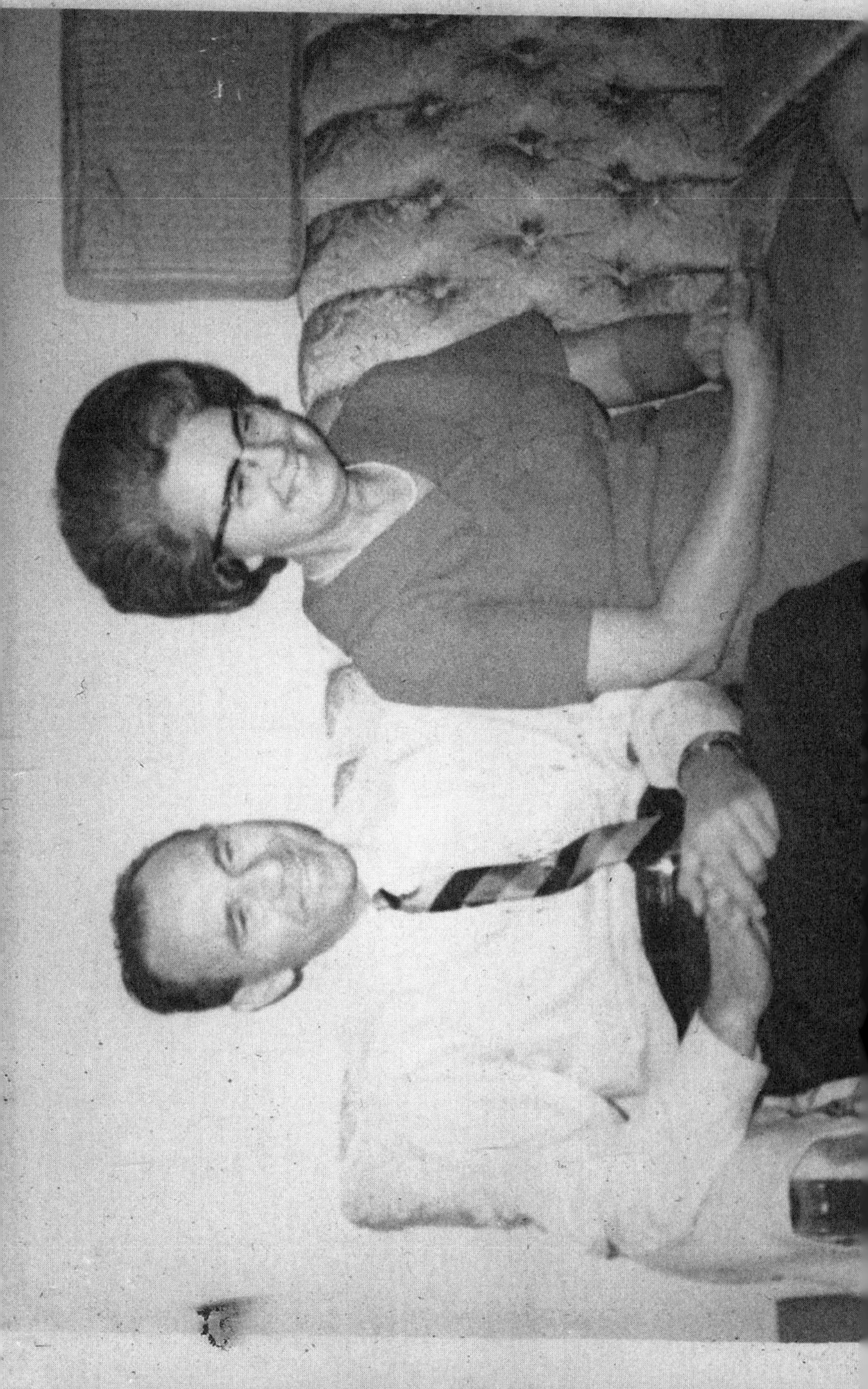

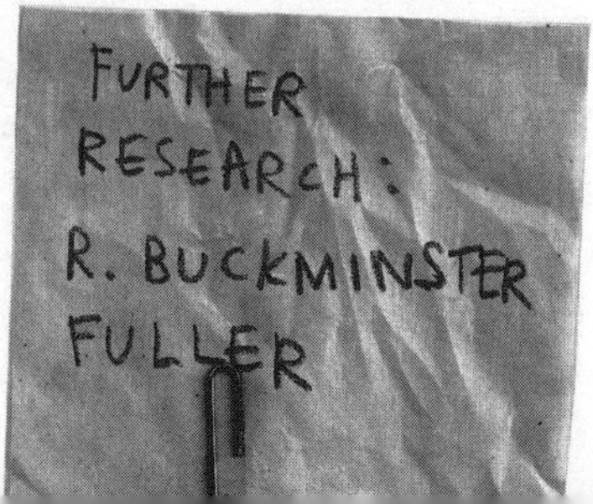
FURTHER
RESEARCH:
R. BUCKMINSTER
FULLER

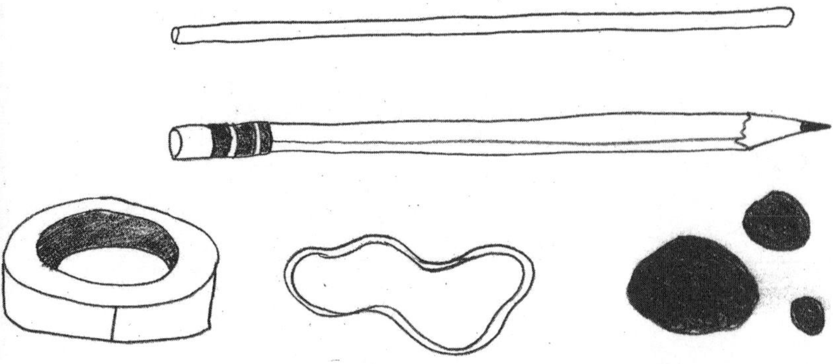

Create an invention using the following objects: a paper bag, a straw, tape, a pencil, an elastic band, and a few rocks.

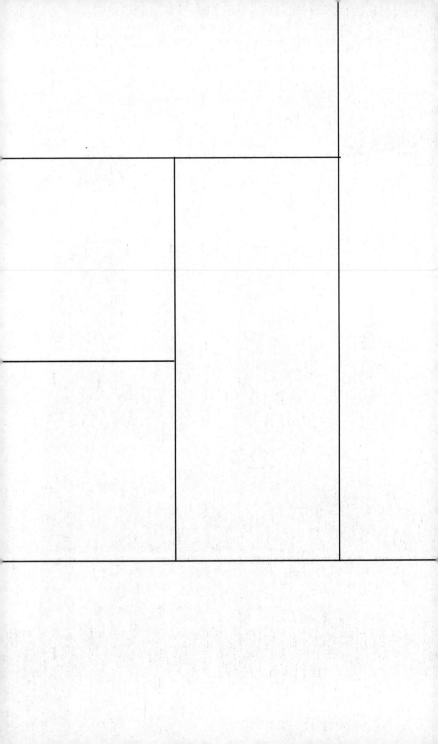

1. Do a pencil rubbing of a series of textures in the boxes (experiment with different materials).
2. Cut out random shapes.
3. Create a collage.

Do a drawing using only tape.

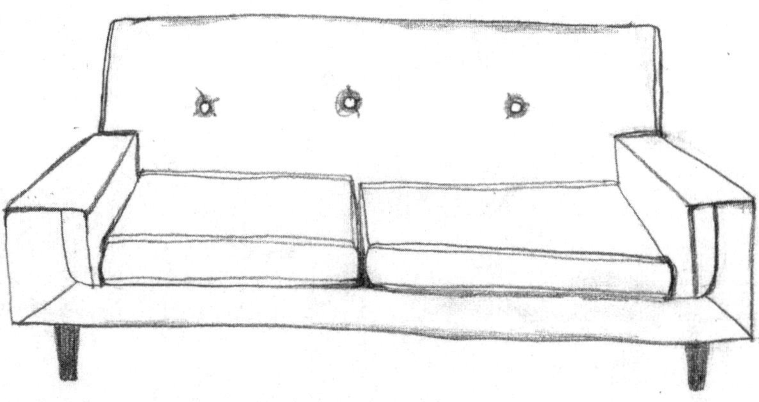

PSYCHOLOGICAL MESS

1. Get comfy.
2. Make a list of all your current problems.

Work with materials that bleed through the paper to the other side (markers, watercolor, pens). Create as much bleed as possible.

Create a face out of garbage and debris you find.

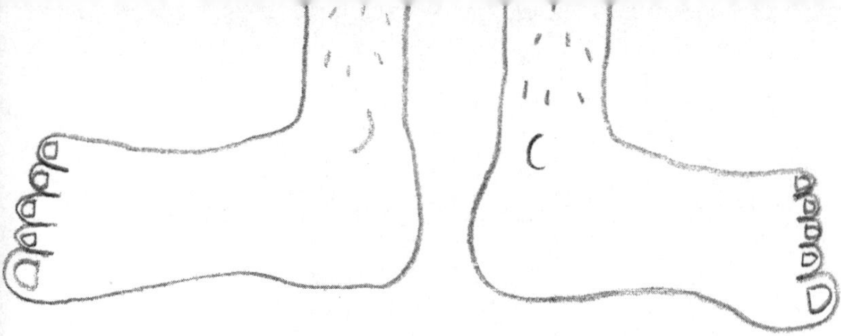

Write with your feet.

1. Cut out the instructions below.
2. Put them in a hat or bowl.
3. Pick them randomly to create a drawing.

CIRCLE IT.	DRAW TEN LINES.	SCRIBBLE WILDLY.	DRAW AN EXPLOSION.
COLOR IT IN.	FILL IN THE PAGE.	WRITE THE FIRST WORD YOU THINK OF.	DO NOTHING.
DRAW A HAT.	DRAW A DOTTED LINE.	DRAW SOMETHING RED.	DRAW A MOUNTAIN.
DRAW A HEAD.	WRITE YOUR FIRST NAME.	DRAW A BOX.	IT IS RAINING.
DRAW A LINE.	DRAW A CIRCLE.	CONNECT THE CORNERS.	DRAW UPSIDE DOWN.
DO IT AGAIN.	COLOR IT IN.	MAKE A HOLE.	ADD A PATTERN.
ERASE IT.	ADD SPOTS.	ADD STRIPES.	ADD SOME TAPE.
USE A MARKER.	COVER IT UP.	DRUM ON THE PAGE.	DRAW VERY LIGHTLY.
MAKE A FACE.	DRAW TEN TRIANGLES.	MAKE A BUMPY LINE.	MAKE LARGE HEAVY STROKES.

THOUGHT MESS

1. Hang many sheets of paper to your wall.
2. For one week write down your random thoughts on the wall.

1. Create a mess with mystery ingredients.
2. Have others try to guess what you used.

Layer this page with as many different materials as you can.

GROUP MESS

Challenge a friend to a mess duel. Find a person to judge. The best mess wins!

Draw or paint with several utensils (pens, pencils, pieces of chalk, etc.) at once.

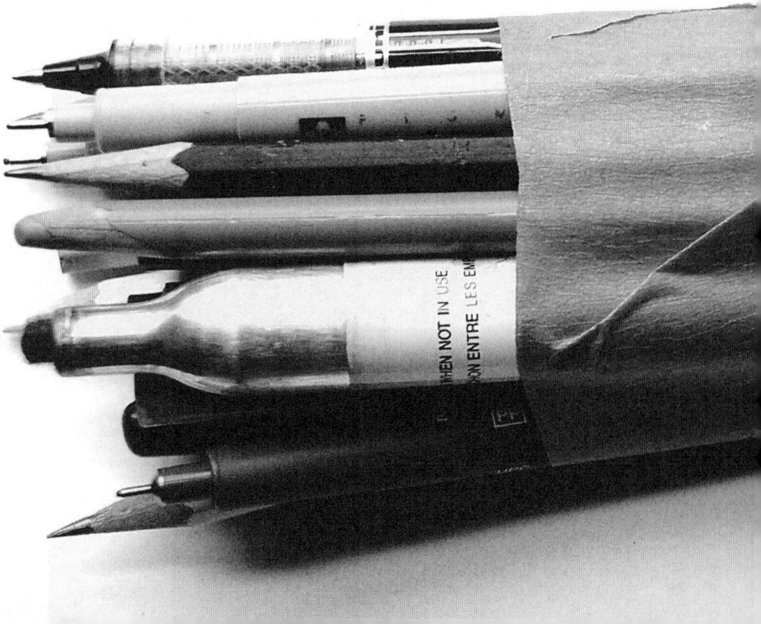

Add 365 lines to this page.
(If you like you can do one a day for a year.)

1. Tie a piece of string to a pencil.
2. Dip the string into some kind of paint or ink.
3. Using the string as a whip, flail the string onto the paper.

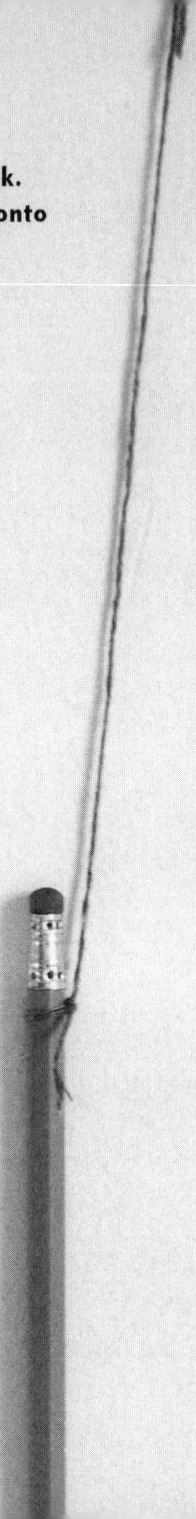

DRAW A CIRCLE...

as if your pen just exploded.
as if your pen was on fire.
as if you had to kill time.
as if you had never drawn before.
as if there was a dog sitting on the middle of the page.
as if you had a terminal illness.
as if you were Picasso.
as if you were stranded on a desert island.
as a nose.
that is a symbol of impermanence.
that is a sun.
that looks like something else.
with corners.
that is a face.
that makes you laugh.
that flies.
you saw today.
from your dreams.
as a piece of furniture.
as a building.
as a sea monster.
that is hidden from view.
that is a portal.
that is life changing.
that scares you.
that has a soft texture.
that has a rough texture.
that makes a statement.
that is portable.
that conceals something.
that tells a story.
that moves.
that talks.
that you can consume.
that is heavy.
that is furry.
that is imaginary.

Do a drawing with a pin.

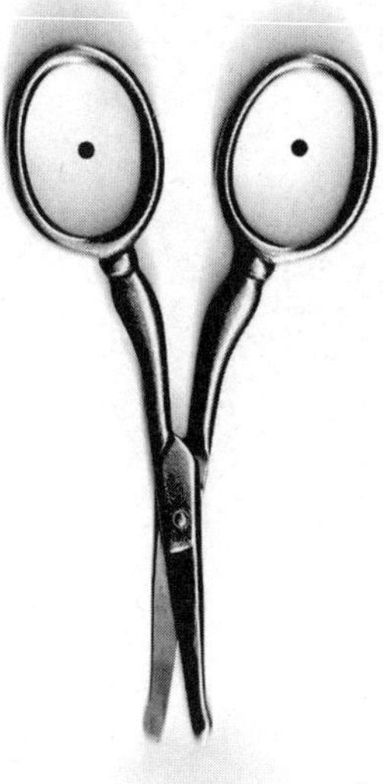

1. Fold page several times.
2. Make random cuttings with scissors.
3. Unfold.
4. Repeat with different folds.

1. **Take an object you have multiples of. (Ideas: plastic bags, leaves, balloons, clothes, dirt.)**
2. **Create a huge mess by throwing the object randomly in the air.**
3. **Photograph it (or create a video).**

How many things can you scrape here?

Write down what they are.

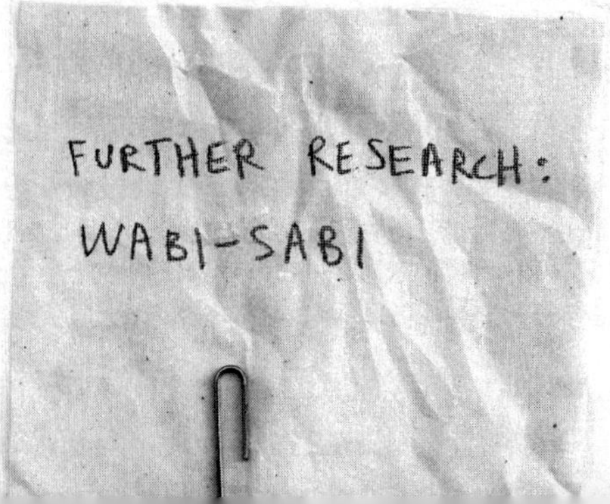
FURTHER RESEARCH:
WABI-SABI

FIELD TRIP: IMPERFECTION

Find several examples of a mess/ imperfection in nature.

Doodle by connecting the dots in an interesting way.

THE MINI ENCYCLOPEDIA

MOVEMENT			
MATERIALS			
WRITING			
SOCIAL INTERACTIONS			
MISC.			

OF MESSES AND MISTAKES

MOVEMENT			
MATERIALS			
WRITING			
SOCIAL INTERACTIONS			
MISC.			

NOTES

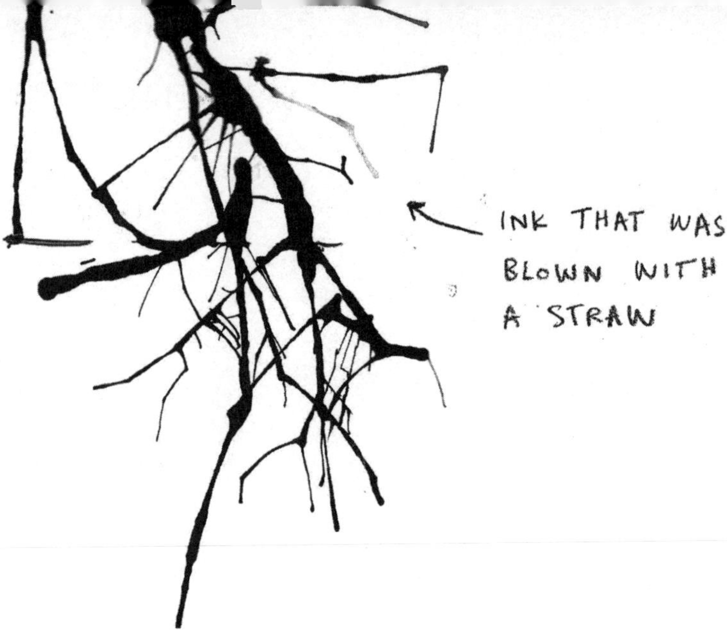

ACKNOWLEDGMENTS

Some of the ideas in this book were influenced by an amazing (long out-of-print) book called *How to Design by Accident* by James F. O'Brien (Dover, 1968), which used a lot of heavy-duty artist materials in creating various textures. My versions rely only on healthy nontoxic materials, most of which you will already have on hand. Thanks also to my husband, Jefferson Pitcher, who once again worked as my model, and to my son, Tilden Pitcher, whose drawing was included in this book (a great artist at the age of two and king of messes). This book would not exist without the inspiring minds of my editor, Meg Leder, and publisher, John Duff, whose suggestions and comments always make my work better. And also to my agent, Faith Hamlin, whose constant support makes me feel completely blessed.

Washing Instructions
Hand wash or gentle cycle
on cold. Lay flat to dry.

THE POCKET SCAVENGER

KERI SMITH

Particular Books

Create a funny character.

PARTICULAR BOOKS

Published by the Penguin Group
Penguin Books Ltd, 80 Strand, London WC2R 0RL, England
Penguin Group (USA) Inc., 375 Hudson Street, New York, New York 10014, USA
Penguin Group (Canada), 90 Eglinton Avenue East, Suite 700, Toronto, Ontario, Canada M4P 2Y3
(a division of Pearson Penguin Canada Inc.)
Penguin Ireland, 25 St Stephen's Green, Dublin 2, Ireland (a division of Penguin Books Ltd)
Penguin Group (Australia), 707 Collins Street, Melbourne, Victoria 3008, Australia
(a division of Pearson Australia Group Pty Ltd)
Penguin Books India Pvt Ltd, 11 Community Centre, Panchsheel Park, New Delhi – 110 017, India
Penguin Group (NZ), 67 Apollo Drive, Rosedale, Auckland 0632, New Zealand
(a division of Pearson New Zealand Ltd)
Penguin Books (South Africa) (Pty) Ltd, Block D, Rosebank Office Park,
181 Jan Smuts Avenue, Parktown North, Gauteng 2193, South Africa

Penguin Books Ltd, Registered Offices: 80 Strand, London WC2R 0RL, England

www.penguin.com

First published by Perigee Books, part of the Penguin Group (USA) Inc. 2013
First published in Great Britain by Particular Books 2013
004

Art and design by Keri Smith

Printed and bound by CPI Group (UK) Ltd, Croydon, CR0 4YY

ISBN: 978-1-846-14709-8

www.greenpenguin.co.uk

MIX
Paper from responsible sources
FSC www.fsc.org FSC™ C018179

Penguin Books is committed to a sustainable future for our business, our readers and our planet. This book is made from Forest Stewardship Council™ certified paper.

ALWAYS LEARNING PEARSON

Make into a building (house).

THIS BOOK BELONGS TO:

WHO IS AN OFFICIAL SCAVENGER AND WORLD EXPLORER.

IF FOUND, PLEASE RETURN TO:

(ADDRESS, EMAIL OR PHONE #)

SCAVENGING LOCATIONS:

CODENAME: ------------------

THIS BOOK IS DEDICATED TO ALL THE WORLD'S GREAT TEACHERS. IT ONLY TAKES ONE TO ALTER THE PATH OF A LIFE!

Combine with something from nature.

CONTENTS

INTRODUCTION

COLLECT & ALTER

Turn into a disguise.

Make into a location on a map.

Conceal it.

SOME EXTRA THINGS

Add polka dots.

A SINGLE INANIMATE OBJECT, USELESS IN ITSELF, CAN BE THE FOCUS OF A WORLD.

-YI-FU TUAN

Remove a section.

DEFINITION OF A SCAVENGER

Scavengers...

- go on mini adventures no matter where they are, especially in the most mundane of circumstances
- notice the ground beneath their feet, prowl the world looking for treasures
- see beauty in simple items, when sometimes others do not
- know that all objects can be imbued with special powers
- are interested in transforming simple objects into works of art
- often have collections of items in the bottom of their bag, scattered about their home, or hidden in a yard somewhere
- are always prepared to collect and will go to great lengths to do so, even occasionally putting themselves in precarious situations

COULD THIS BE YOU?

If so, proceed to the next section.

Add stripes.

Scribble on top.

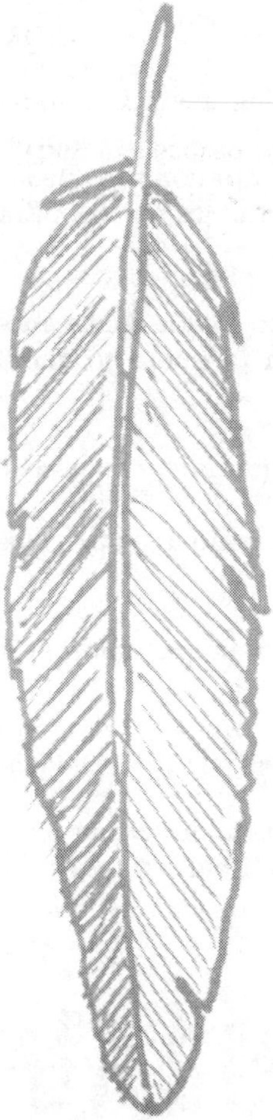

INTRODUCTION

You are invited to go on an adventure—right now, wherever you are.

In the following pages, I'm going to ask you to search for a bunch of items. At first glance, these may seem like simple, mundane, inconsequential things, but don't be fooled—they are of utmost importance!

Every minute of the day there are hundreds (or thousands) of things around us that we don't notice. Our eyes tune them out because they don't seem important for our current needs. But what if we look at every "thing" as if we have never seen it before? As if we do not know its function? In that way, we learn to see it with new eyes.

These things can become very useful if we choose to think of them as raw materials. They are sacred objects just waiting to be collected by a modern-day explorer and used in a variety of artistic experiments.

That is your challenge: to infuse your daily excursions with a quest to see these things with new eyes.

Duplicate it (make a copy).

THE SCAVENGE

The first stage in becoming a natural navigator is to master observation, and the first lesson in this area is that observation is not all about the eyes. And even when it is about the eyes, there is more to it than meets our eyes.
—Tristan Gooley, The Natural Navigator

Most of us have participated in scavenger hunts at some point in our lives: running around a location frantically looking for a set of items typed on a list of some kind, locating the objects before someone else does, finding everything as fast possible.

With the scavenges in this book, we are going to take the act of scavenging into a slightly different realm by first collecting objects and then altering them.

For the first mission, you are going to collect a number of items. They can be found in your immediate environment, on your way to work or school, while you are waiting for the bus, at your local park, while on a hike, while on vacation, and so on. Use the checklist at the back of this book for a quick reference of what to scavenge. For the purposes of this book, you can choose the speed at which you perform the scavenge. You may choose to do it alone. Or you can enlist friends and make it a race.

Fold, cut into pieces, and rearrange.

THE ALTERATION

Once you have an item and are ready for the next step, you will turn the book upside down, flip randomly to a page, read the instruction at the top, and alter the item as instructed. (This is referred to as using "chance" because you do not actively get to choose what alteration you are using. The process of flipping causes you to choose without looking at the alteration first.)

These alterations will allow you to create something entirely new. Think of them as a selection of possibilities for outcomes different than what you would have done if you were given a choice. The alterations are where your genius will come in. Each alteration will be interpreted differently by each person. There is no right or wrong or good or bad in terms of how the alteration is performed. You might love the results; you might find them uninteresting. That is part of the fun—not knowing what will occur.

Turn into an article of clothing.

CHANCE:

1. the occurrence and development of events in the absence of any obvious design : he met his brother by chance | what a lucky chance that you are here. 2. the unplanned and unpredictable course of events regarded as a power : chance was offering me success.

A BRIEF HISTORY OF CHANCE

The use of chance in art began in the 1950s with the artists Ellsworth Kelly, François Morellet, and John Cage. These artists used a variety of methods and techniques including the I Ching, grid systems (assigning random colors to the squares), dot systems, random sampling on a computer, dice, using gravity (falling, dropping, dripping), chance meetings, etc.

Trace it and use the shape as basis for a new drawing.

So often when we are creating something—a piece of art, a piece of writing, a musical composition—we do what has worked for us in the past, what we are the best at, what is current, what is reliable, what is obvious, what we think is good. But this method tends to make our work repetitive and stale. Creativity arises from our ability to see things from many different angles. New connections (things that have not been connected before) create new ideas.

Incorporating chance into the exercise allows us to make connections and try things that we might not have done on our own. We are forced out of our habitual ways of thinking or acting.

Chance is beloved of Art, and Art of Chance.

–Agathon, fragments (c. 415 B.C.), quoted by Aristotle

Make it pretty.

THE BENEFITS AND JOYS OF BEING A SCAVENGER

I devote a day to creating a kind of "story." Walking down, say, Sixth Avenue, I'll suddenly see something that intrigues me—a plastic bag, a green umbrella, an airplane tracing a line in the sky. That's how I get started.
—Gabriel Orozco (on recent films, 1998)

1. The process of collecting tunes us into our environment and makes use of our increasingly underused senses. You may begin to see that everything is interesting.

2. In our current culture of immediacy, we have lost the experience of "the quest," the search for that elusive item and the stories we create in our attempt to find it. These stories, the process (vs. the object itself), are often what make life interesting.

3. Scavenging is fun and addictive (and much better for us than watching screens all day), especially when done with others and when you share your unique results.

4. Living in a consumerist society, it is easy to get caught up in a lifestyle that is just about shopping or is connected to a corporate entity. This leaves us feeling empty and causes a discon-

Combine with page 14.

nect with the natural world. It is important for us to participate in activities that open us up to exploring the world around us on a regular basis without a focus on money/commerce. Tuning into our immediate environment also serves to make us feel more connected to the natural world.

5. You will never be at a loss for materials for artistic endeavors.

What if we begin to see the world as alive and animate? What if every item told a story?

With The Pocket Scavenger, what emerges will be entirely different for every person who works with the book. Each version will be based on a variety of factors, our life experiences, our location, our culture, chance, and how we interpret the ideas. Working with items in this way will help train our brains to look at things without preconceived ideas. Over time we will naturally make new connections and formulate new patterns of thinking. We will develop a habit of "trying something new" or different.

AN IMPORTANT NOTE:

SOMETIMES THE RESULT WILL BE INTERESTING AND SOMETIMES IT WON'T. THAT IS THE NATURE OF AN EXPERIMENT.

Clean it up.

SCAVENGER TOOLS

YOU WILL NEED:

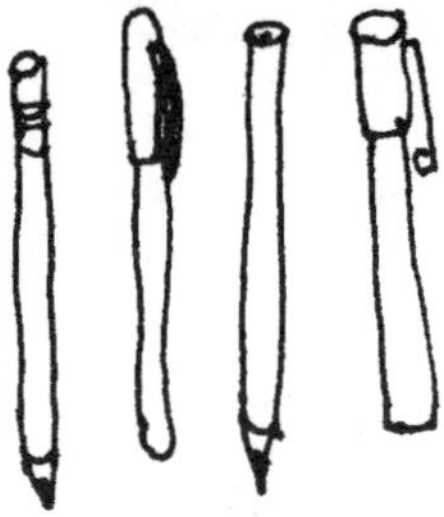

ERASER

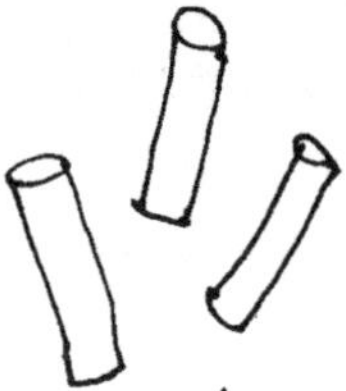

CHALK

SCISSOR

PAINT

A VARIETY OF WRITING AND DRAWING UTENSILS

A SELECTION OF ART MATERIALS

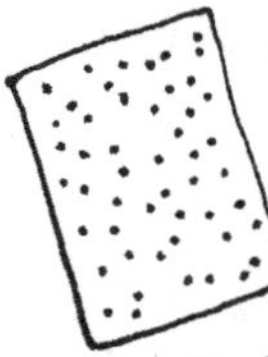

COFFEE
TEA

SAND PAPER

NEWSPAPER

MUD

SOME NON-ART MATERIALS*

* SEE LIST OF ALTERATION MATERIALS ON THE NEXT PAGE.

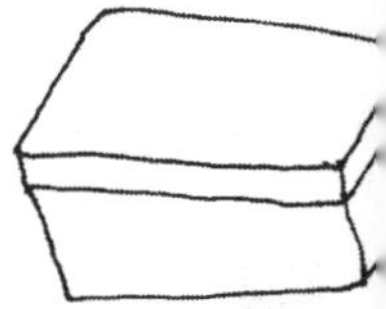

VARIOUS WAYS TO STORE THINGS UNTIL YOU CAN AFFIX THEM INTO THE BOOK. ATTACH AN ENVELOPE TO THE INSIDE OF THE BACK COVER TO STORE THINGS TEMPORARILY WHEN YOU ARE OUT ON SCAVENGES.

Add a mess.

A "SCAVENGING UNIFORM" OF SOME KIND, SOMETHING THAT HELPS GET YOU INTO THE MIND-SET.

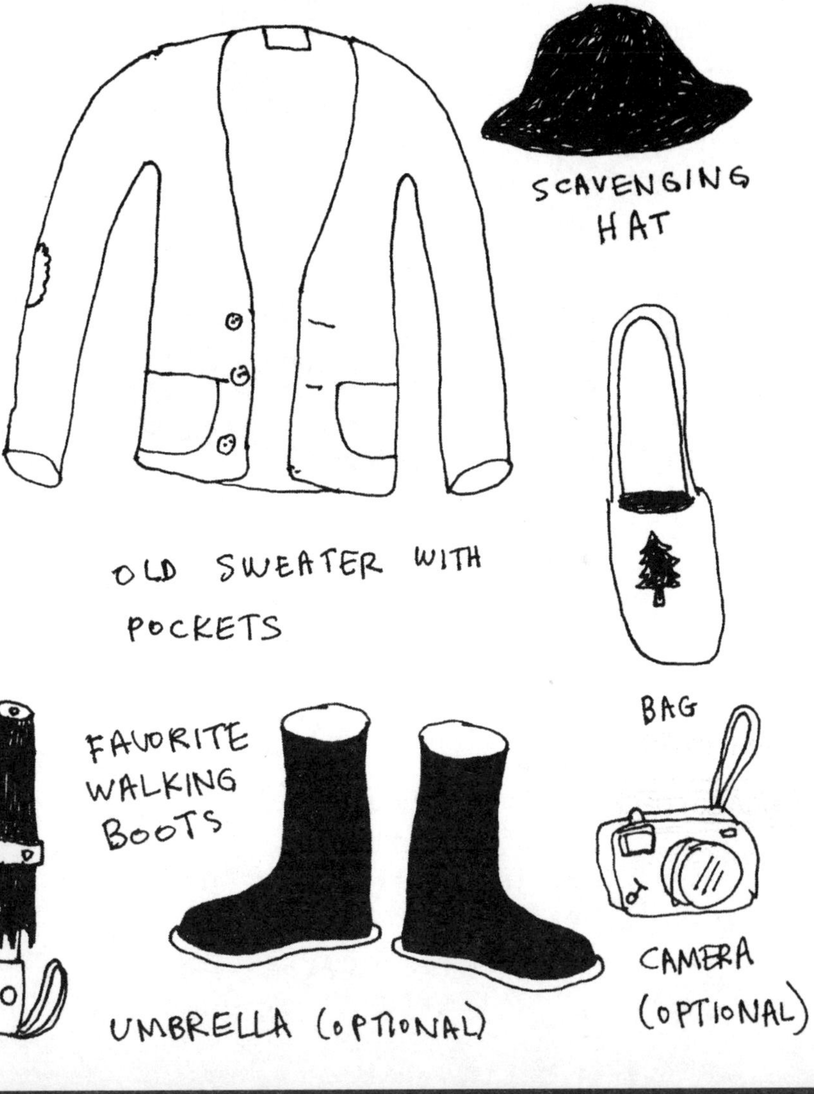

Turn it upside down. What does it look like now?

ATTACHMENT METHODS:

NOTE: SOME ITEMS MAY SEEM A LITTLE BULKY FOR THE BOOK. THIS IS TO BE EXPECTED. YOU MAY HAVE TO PUT A LARGE ELASTIC BAND AROUND IT TO KEEP IT CONTAINED.

ALTERATION MATERIALS YOU MAY LIKE TO USE...

SCAVENGING TIPS

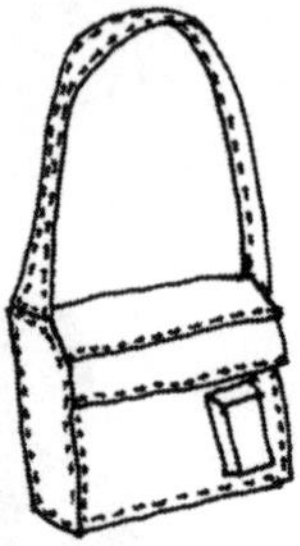

- Get in the habit of looking around while wandering in your neighborhood. Scan the ground for finds. Some things you will find quickly, or know exactly where to look. Others will take some time and require ingenuity and serendipity. Occasionally you will come upon something when you least expect it (e.g., while walking to work, you spot a piece of red string on the sidewalk); these are the most interesting finds and make the best stories. Write about it on the object's page.

- Recruit your friends and family to help you (if you choose).

- Enjoy the process. Scavenging works best when you are fully immersed in the moment.

- Memorize (or familiarize) yourself with the list of items to scavenge, so you will be working on it as you go about your day.

- Try navigating your environment in a non-linear fashion, or take different routes than you normally do. You may discover new things this way.

IMPORTANT NOTE: You will want to avoid any items that are sharp, dangerous-looking, or toxic. (Avoid standing water or unknown substances.) If you are unsure if an item is okay, it is best to leave it behind.

Add some kind of explosion.

ALTERATION TIPS

- Be willing to try something just to see what happens—even if you don't think you will like it. You may come up with the most interesting stuff this way! Get into the habit of experimenting.

- If you come upon a wild card you may pick an alteration of your choosing, or you can just flip again.

- Try working with as many different materials as you can. So for example, if the alteration says "add dots" you could use paint, coffee, gum, collage, or anything else you can think of!

- If you are prone to cheating, dare yourself to do as instructed.

- If you really dislike what you created, you have permission to repeat the whole process or transform it into something else entirely.

Bonus tip: You may like to use the alterations in this book for other projects you are working on.

Add warmth.

INSTRUCTIONS

1. Take this book with you everywhere you go.

2. Find/collect the things on each page. Affix them somehow to the left-hand side of the page.* Fill in the notes about where you found the item. Under "story" you can describe the circumstances surrounding the scavenge.** You may also choose to write an imaginary story about the item.

3. For each collected item, turn the book upside down and randomly flip to a page. Alter it as directed. How you interpret each alteration is up to you.

4. Share your alterations with others using your preferred method (social network, art show, trade book with friends, etc.).

*You may also choose to take photos of the items, but you must find a way to print them so you can alter them later.

**Remember that these items may not seem that important on their own, but in your collecting of them, they will become valuable treasures. You will become the envy of all your friends!

Group several items together.

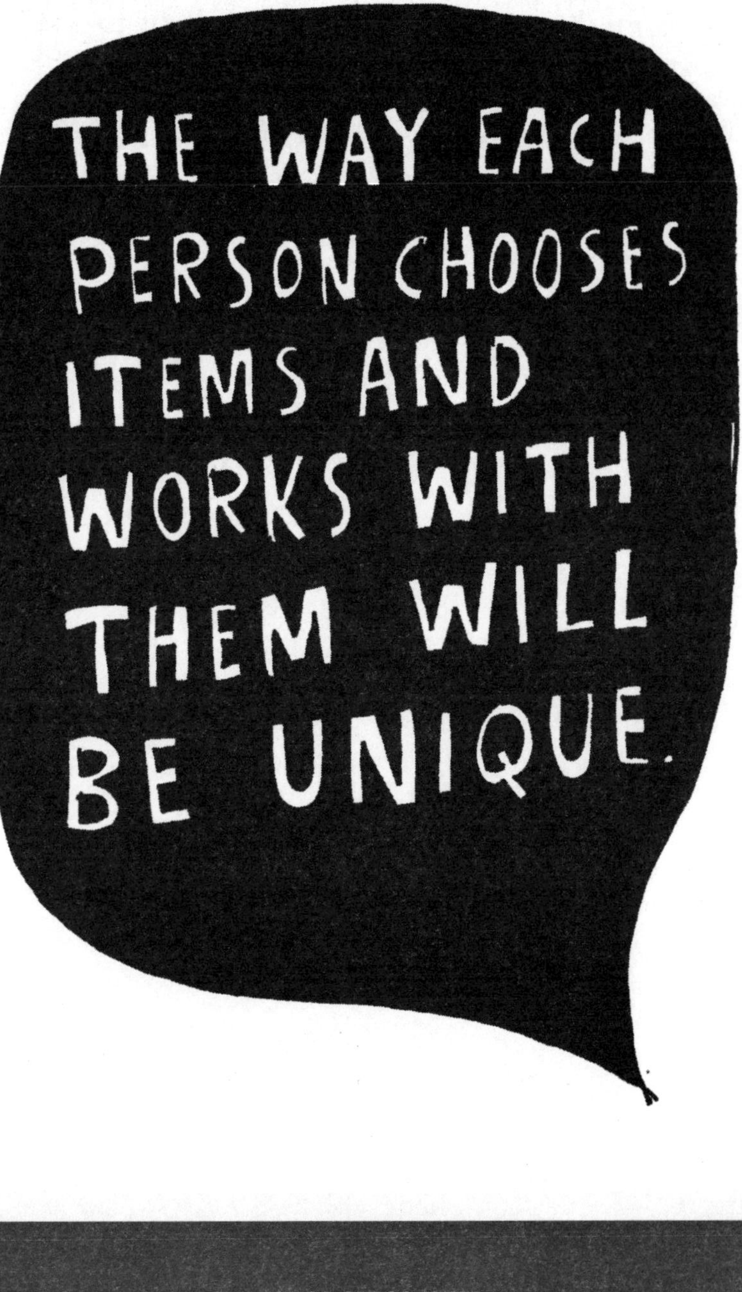
THE WAY EACH PERSON CHOOSES ITEMS AND WORKS WITH THEM WILL BE UNIQUE.

Add some text.

SCAVENGER MAP

Draw a detailed map of your neighborhood. Document on the map all of the locations at which you found your scavenged items. Create your own legend.

Destroy it.

Simplify it.

It's a hat.

1

POSTAGE STAMPS

LOCATION FOUND: ____________

TIME: ______ DATE: ________

STORY: ____________

Flip three pages ahead—follow those directions.

Do nothing.

2

THE NUMBER FIVE

5

LOCATION FOUND: ____________

TIME: ______ DATE: ________

STORY: ____________________

Alter the edges.

Make item the background for something else.

4

3

PAPER CLIP

LOCATION FOUND: ____________

TIME: ______ DATE: ________

STORY: ____________________

Wild card. Choose an alteration yourself.

Add some texture.

4

A FEATHER

LOCATION FOUND: ______________

TIME: ______ DATE: __________

STORY: ______________________

____

____

____

____

____

____

____

____

____

____

Make holes.

Ask a friend what you should do.

5

A USED ENVELOPE

LOCATION FOUND: ____________

TIME: ______ DATE: ________

STORY: ______________

Add legs.

Cut into strips.

6

A TICKET

LOCATION FOUND: ____________

TIME: ______ DATE: ________

STORY: ____________________

____

____

____

____

____

____

____

____

____

____

Combine with a photo.

Add ten colors.

7

NINE CIRCLES

LOCATION FOUND: ____________

TIME: ______ DATE: ________

STORY: ____________________

____

____

____

____

____

____

____

____

____

____

Invent an animal.

Make a self-portrait.

8

A FORM OF CURRENCY

LOCATION FOUND: ______________

TIME: ________ DATE: __________

STORY: ____________________

____

____

____

____

____

____

____

____

____

____

Alter the space around the item (not the item itself).

Add a series of diverging lines.

9

SOMETHING YOU CAN SEE THROUGH

LOCATION FOUND: ____________________

TIME: ________ DATE: ______________

STORY: ____________________________

____

____

____

____

____

____

____

____

____

____

Add a color you dislike.

Fill the entire space.

10

THREE DIFFERENT TEXTURES

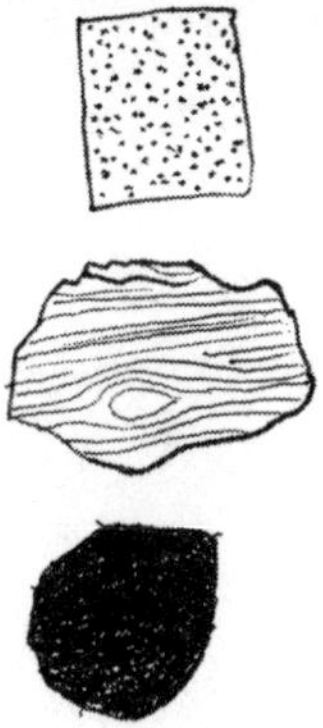

LOCATION FOUND: ____________________

TIME: ________ DATE: ____________

STORY: ____________________

____

____

____

____

____

____

____

____

____

____

Frame it.

20

Add transparent/translucent layers.

The magician's underwear has just been found in a cardboard suitcase floating in a stagnant pond on the outskirts of

11

SOMETHING WITH TEXT ON IT

LOCATION FOUND: ____________

TIME: ________ DATE: ________

STORY: ____________

Delete the middle.

Do something your hero would do.

12

A POST-IT NOTE

LOCATION FOUND: ____________

TIME: ______ DATE: ________

STORY: ______________

Smudge something over it with your fingers.

Crumple it.

13

A PIECE OF MOSS

LOCATION FOUND: ______________

TIME: ________ DATE: __________

STORY: ________________________

____

____

____

____

____

____

____

____

____

____

Soak with water.

Add scratches.

14

SOME WIRE

LOCATION FOUND: ______________

TIME: ________ DATE: __________

STORY: ________________________

Add a series of triangles.

Turn into a landscape.

15

A PART OF SOMETHING YOU ATE

LOCATION FOUND: ______________

TIME: ______ DATE: ______________

STORY: ______________

____

____

____

____

____

____

____

____

____

____

Draw a box.

30

Place in a location where it will get dirty.

16

SOMETHING YOU CAN ONLY FIND IN YOUR LOCAL ENVIRONMENT ?

LOCATION FOUND: ______________

TIME: ______ DATE: ________

STORY: ________________________

____

____

____

____

____

____

____

____

____

____

Lose the item.

Drip coffee or tea on it.

17

SOMETHING ON YOUR BODY

LOCATION FOUND: ____________

TIME: ______ DATE: ________

STORY: ________________

Drip paint on it.

Make it funny.

18

A USED TEA BAG

LOCATION FOUND: ________

TIME: ______ DATE: ______

STORY: ________

____

____

____

____

____

____

____

____

____

____

Scribble with your eyes closed.

Chop it up.

19

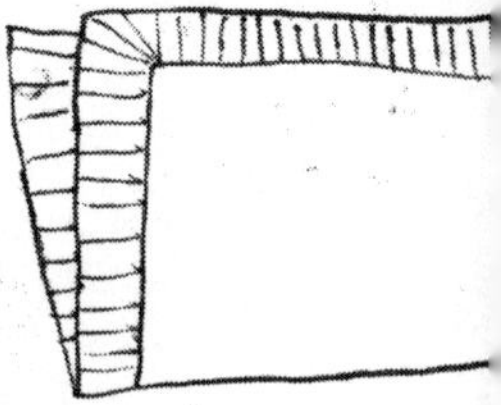

A NAPKIN

LOCATION FOUND: ____________

TIME: ______ DATE: ________

STORY: ________________

Make it political.

Make it obscured.

20

SOMETHING STICKY

LOCATION FOUND: ____________

TIME: ______ DATE: ________

STORY: ______________________

____

____

____

____

____

____

____

____

____

____

Add string.

Turn it into something else.

21

SIX BLUE THINGS

LOCATION FOUND: ____________

TIME: ______ DATE: ________

STORY: ____________________

____

____

____

____

____

____

____

____

____

____

Change the perspective.

Turn it into something you love.

22

A PIECE OF A PUZZLE

LOCATION FOUND: ____________

TIME: ______ DATE: ________

STORY: ____________________

____

____

____

____

____

____

____

____

____

____

Drag it along a rough surface.

Smear something onto it.

23

AN ELASTIC BAND

LOCATION FOUND: ______________

TIME: ______ DATE: __________

STORY: ____________________

____

____

____

____

____

____

____

____

____

____

Cut out some bits of paper. Glue them on.

Add some thumbprints.

24

AN IMAGE OF A CHARACTER

LOCATION FOUND: ____________

TIME: ______ DATE: ________

STORY: ____________________

____

____

____

____

____

____

____

____

____

____

Add circles.

Draw the opposite.

25

SEVERAL KINDS OF LEAVES

LOCATION FOUND: ______________

TIME: ________ DATE: ____________

STORY: ____________________________

____

____

____

____

____

____

____

____

____

____

Consider it complete.

Turn it into a story.

26

A PIECE OF RED STRING

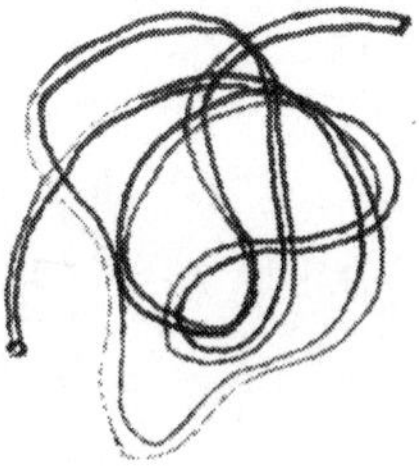

LOCATION FOUND: ______________

TIME: ________ DATE: __________

STORY: ______________________

____

____

____

____

____

____

____

____

____

____

What sound would it make?

Turn it into a vehicle.

27

A WRAPPER

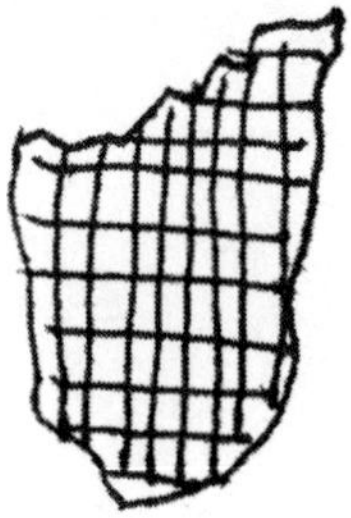

LOCATION FOUND: ____________

TIME: ______ DATE: ________

STORY: ____________________

____

____

____

____

____

____

____

____

____

____

Frame it.

Age it.

28

A PHOTO OF YOURSELF

LOCATION FOUND: ____________

TIME: ______ DATE: ________

STORY: ____________________

Wild card. Choose an alteration yourself.

Add eyes.

THERE ARE SO MANY JOYS, AND I HAVE ONLY KNOWN THE ONES THAT COME LIKE A MIRACLE AND TOUCH ORDINARY LIFE WITH LIGHT. ANAÏS NIN

29

A POSTCARD

LOCATION FOUND: ____________

TIME: ______ DATE: ________

STORY: ____________

Add tape.

58

Color outside the lines.

30

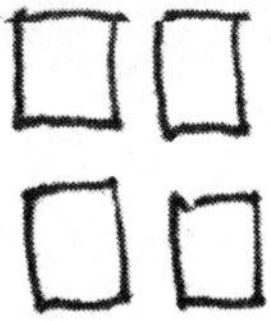

FOUR SQUARES

LOCATION FOUND: ____________

TIME: ________ DATE: ____________

STORY: ____________________

____

____

____

____

____

____

____

____

____

____

Add some music.

Make it REALLY funny.

31

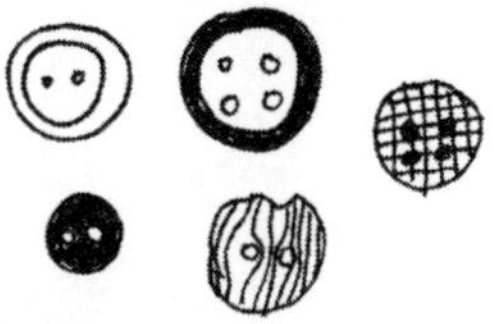

FIVE BUTTONS

LOCATION FOUND: ______________

TIME: ________ DATE: ________

STORY: ______________________

____

____

____

____

____

____

____

____

____

____

Turn it into a math equation.

Turn it into a pattern (repeat it).

32

AN IMAGE OF AN ELEPHANT

LOCATION FOUND: ________________

TIME: ________ DATE: ____________

STORY: ________________________

____

____

____

____

____

____

____

____

____

____

Attach something else.

Add a newspaper clipping.

33

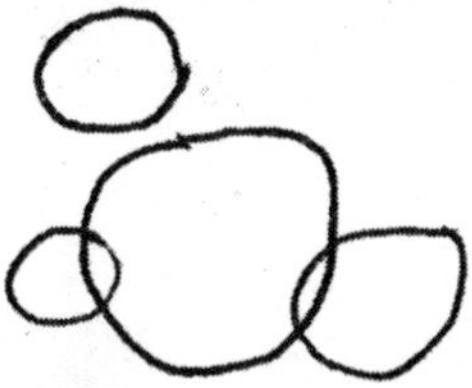

ROCK TRACINGS

LOCATION FOUND: ____________

TIME: ______ DATE: ________

STORY: ____________________

____

____

____

____

____

____

____

____

____

____

Spatter it.

Stencil something over top (a word or a shape).

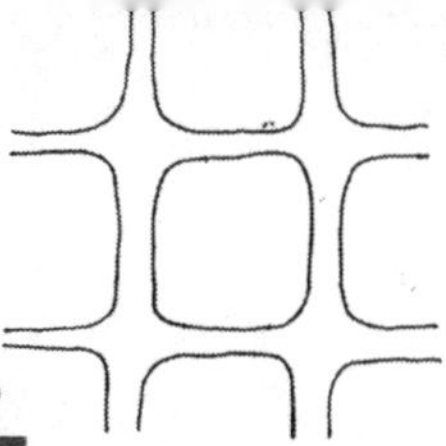

34

SOMETHING ORANGE

LOCATION FOUND: ____________

TIME: ______ DATE: ________

STORY: ____________________

Add fog.

Add exactly six lines/marks.

35

SOMETHING FROM THE YEAR YOU WERE BORN

LOCATION FOUND: ____________

TIME: ______ DATE: ________

STORY: ____________________

Add a grid.

Cover with chalk. Remove some.

36

YOU HAVE A FLANNEL UNDERSHIRT.

A HANDWRITTEN QUOTE

LOCATION FOUND: ____________

TIME: ______ DATE: ________

STORY: ____________

Play.

Scratch.

72

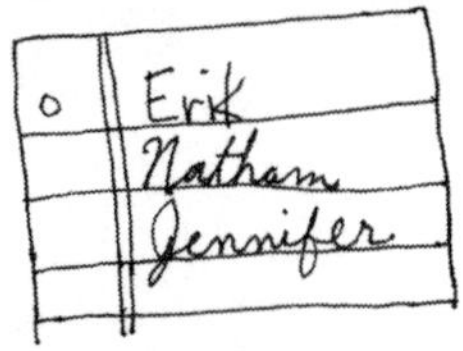

37

SAMPLES OF HANDWRITING FROM FIVE DIFFERENT PEOPLE

LOCATION FOUND: ______________

TIME: ________ DATE: __________

STORY: ______________________

Add one never-ending line.

38

A PENCIL RUBBING OF A GRAVESTONE

LOCATION FOUND: ____________

TIME: ________ DATE: ________

STORY: ______________________

____

____

____

____

____

____

____

____

____

____

What memory does it spark? Write about it.

Turn into an adventure.

39

A HAIR SAMPLE

LOCATION FOUND: ____________

TIME: ______ DATE: ________

STORY: ______________________

____

____

____

____

____

____

____

____

____

____

Add a shadow.

Write five questions about the item.

40

YOU WILL SOON MAKE A FRIEND.

A FORTUNE FROM A FORTUNE COOKIE

LOCATION FOUND: ____________

TIME: ______ DATE: ________

STORY: ______________

____

____

____

____

____

____

____

____

____

____

Add some very tiny, almost imperceptible decoration.

Turn into a badge.

41

COUPON
#0-14-130 115-5
GREETINGS TO YOU, THE
LUCKY FINDER OF THIS COUPON.

A COUPON

LOCATION FOUND: ____________

TIME: ______ DATE: ________

STORY: ____________________

Turn into a magical object.

82

Wild card. Choose an alteration yourself.

42

SOMETHING THAT IS BROKEN OR DAMAGED

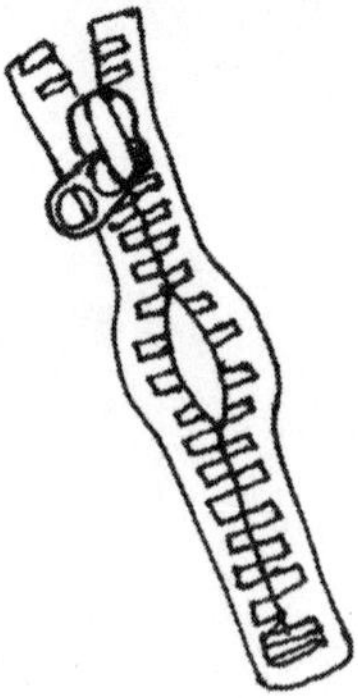

LOCATION FOUND: ____________

TIME: ______ DATE: ________

STORY: ________________

____

____

____

____

____

____

____

____

____

____

Invent a story.

dd a color based on a memory association with the item.

43

SOMETHING THAT WAS DISCARDED

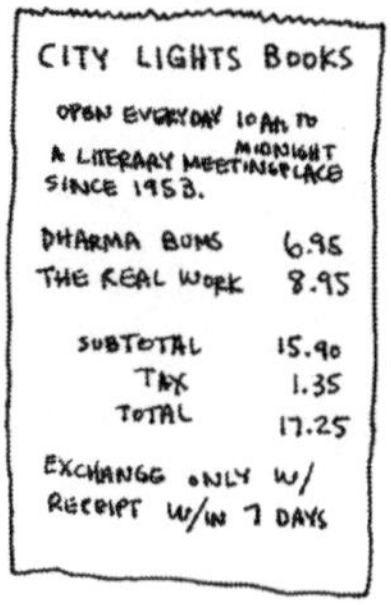
CITY LIGHTS BOOKS
OPEN EVERYDAY 10AM TO MIDNIGHT
A LITERARY MEETINGPLACE SINCE 1953.
DHARMA BUMS 6.95
THE REAL WORK 8.95
SUBTOTAL 15.90
TAX 1.35
TOTAL 17.25
EXCHANGE ONLY W/ RECEIPT W/IN 7 DAYS

LOCATION FOUND: ____________

TIME: ______ DATE: ________

STORY: ______________

Do something strange.

98

Write an ode to this item.

44

A STAIN MADE BY A LIQUID

LOCATION FOUND: ______________

TIME: ______ DATE: __________

STORY: ____________________

____

____

____

____

____

____

____

____

____

____

Combine with another found item.

Add your favorite color in abundance.

45

A STAIN THAT IS GREEN

LOCATION FOUND: ______________

TIME: ________ DATE: __________

STORY: ________________________

Alter item in a way that makes you happy.

Add a pattern.

46

SOMETHING THAT CAN BE CRUMBLED

LOCATION FOUND: ____________

TIME: ______ DATE: ________

STORY: ______________________

Turn into a floorplan.

Combine with a leaf.

47

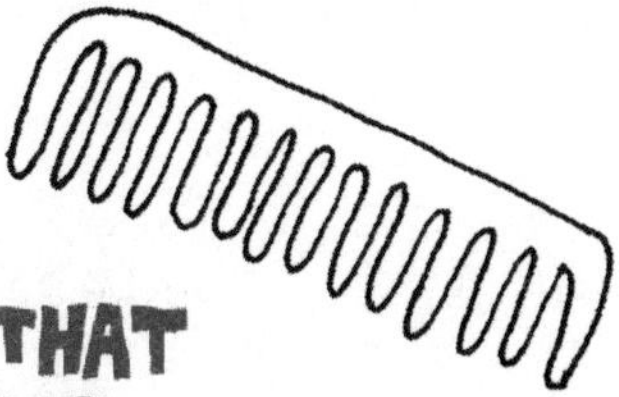

SOMETHING THAT CAN BE DRAGGED AND LEAVES A MARK

LOCATION FOUND: ____________________

TIME: __________ DATE: ______________

STORY: ______________________________

____

____

____

____

____

____

____

____

____

____

Add some cracks.

Add stitches.

48

SOMETHING THAT WAS PART OF A TREE

LOCATION FOUND: ______________

TIME: ______ DATE: __________

STORY: ____________________

____

____

____

____

____

____

____

____

____

____

Add some triangles.

Make it inviting.

49

SOMETHING THAT WAS PLANTED

LOCATION FOUND: ______________

TIME: ________ DATE: __________

STORY: ______________________

____

____

____

____

____

____

____

____

____

____

Make it dark.

Connect this item to an item you love.

50

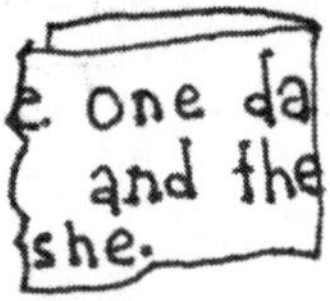

A FOUND NOTE

LOCATION FOUND: ____________

TIME: ______ DATE: ________

STORY: ______________________

____

____

____

____

____

____

____

____

____

____

Dream up a scenario.

100

Take in a different direction.

51

A PIECE OF FLAT CANDY

LOCATION FOUND: ____________

TIME: ______ DATE: ________

STORY: ________________________

____

____

____

____

____

____

____

____

____

____

What would you have done at age five?

Add another dimension.

52

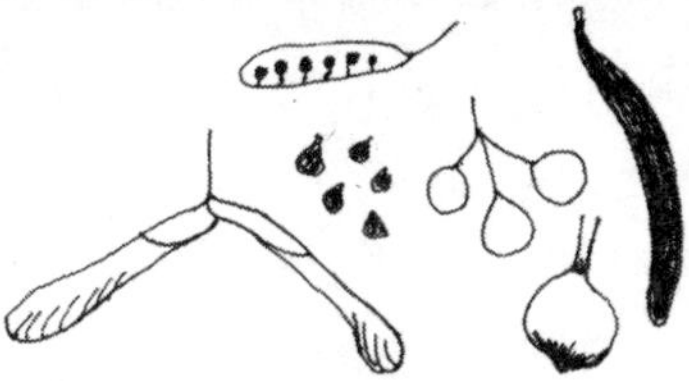

A FEW SEED PODS

LOCATION FOUND: ____________

TIME: ______ DATE: __________

STORY: ____________

Rearrange.

Drip and blow ink.

53

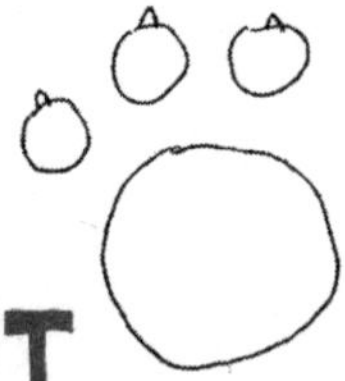

SOMETHING LEFT BY AN ANIMAL

LOCATION FOUND: ____________

TIME: ______ DATE: ________

STORY: ________________

Wrinkle.

Cut in half.

54

SOMETHING THAT WAS CREATED USING A MACHINE

LOCATION FOUND: ____________

TIME: ______ DATE: ________

STORY: ____________________

____

____

____

____

____

____

____

____

____

____

Paint with your finger.

Drop string that has ink on it (make a print).

55

What story down there awaits its end?

SOMETHING THAT WAS MADE BY HAND

LOCATION FOUND: ____________

TIME: ______ DATE: ________

STORY: ________________

Rub surface with dirt.

Squirt ink (or another colored liquid).

56

SOMETHING THAT IS MINIATURE

LOCATION FOUND: ____________

TIME: ______ DATE: ________

STORY: _________________

Paint it red.

Add several blobs of glue.

57

A PIECE OF ORIGAMI

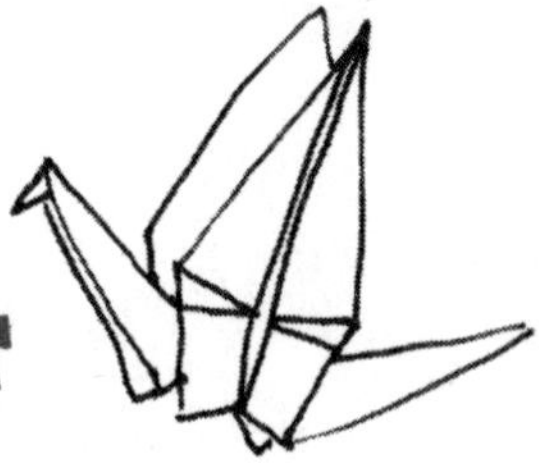

LOCATION FOUND: ______________

TIME: ________ DATE: __________

STORY: ________________________

____

____

____

____

____

____

____

____

____

____

Wild card. Choose an alteration yourself.

Turn into a monster.

58

SOMETHING THAT WAS GIVEN TO YOU

LOCATION FOUND: ____________________

TIME: ________ DATE: ____________

STORY: ______________________________

____

____

____

____

____

____

____

____

____

____

Add a pencil rubbing texture.

59

A DRAWING (NOT DONE BY YOU)

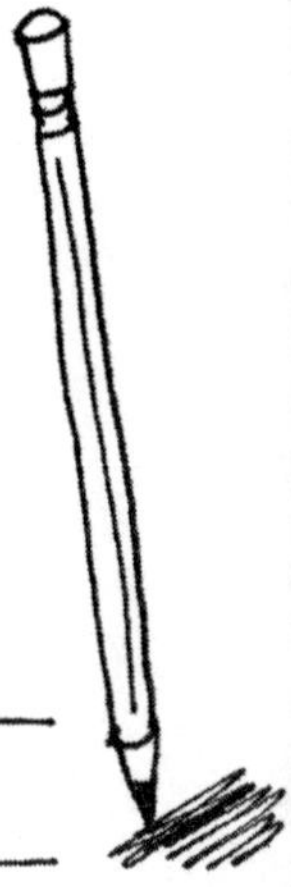

LOCATION FOUND: ______________

TIME: ________ DATE: ________

STORY: ______________

____

____

____

____

____

____

____

____

____

____

Add something that is blown across the surface.

Turn into an island.

60

SEVERAL DIFFERENT KINDS OF GRASS

LOCATION FOUND: ____________

TIME: ______ DATE: ________

STORY: ____________________

____

____

____

____

____

____

____

____

____

____

Alter the shape.

Print something onto it.

61

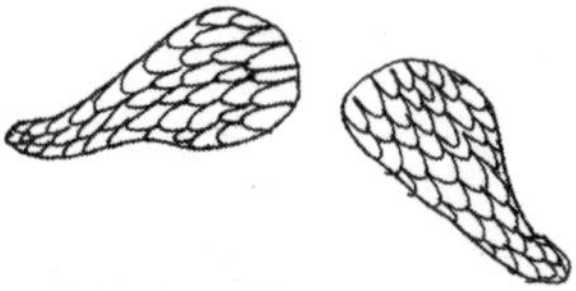

SOMETHING THAT IS IMAGINARY

LOCATION FOUND: ____________

TIME: ______ DATE: ________

STORY: ____________________

____

____

____

____

____

____

____

____

____

____

Make it into a boat.

Combine several alterations of your choosing.

62

A PIECE OF STYROFOAM

LOCATION FOUND: ______________

TIME: ________ DATE: ________

STORY: ______________________

____

____

____

____

____

____

____

____

____

____

Do something really fast without thinking.

Turn it into a machine/device.

63

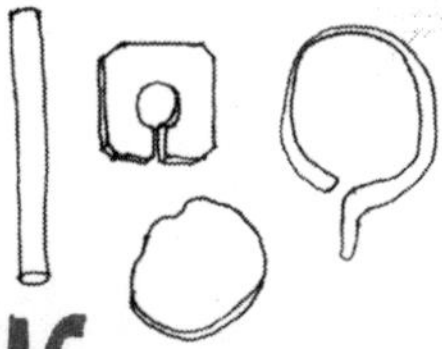

SEVERAL PLASTIC ITEMS OF DIFFERENT COLORS

LOCATION FOUND: ____________

TIME: ______ DATE: ________

STORY: ____________

Add a grid.

Add some movement.

64

SOMETHING WITH SPOTS

LOCATION FOUND: ____________

TIME: ______ DATE: ________

STORY: ________________

____

____

____

____

____

____

____

____

____

____

Let your gut tell you what to do.

Draw in the same direction as the wind.

65

SOMETHING CURVED

LOCATION FOUND: ____________

TIME: ______ DATE: ________

STORY: ____________________

Add colored paper.

Do some crosshatching.

66

SIX TRIANGLES

LOCATION FOUND: ____________

TIME: ______ DATE: ________

STORY: ____________________

Add an explosion.

Draw it as you see it.

67

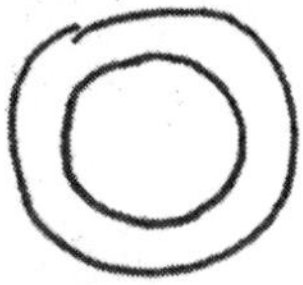

SOMETHING WITH A HOLE IN IT

LOCATION FOUND: ____________

TIME: ______ DATE: ________

STORY: ____________________

Add your favorite shape.

Turn it into a sign.

68

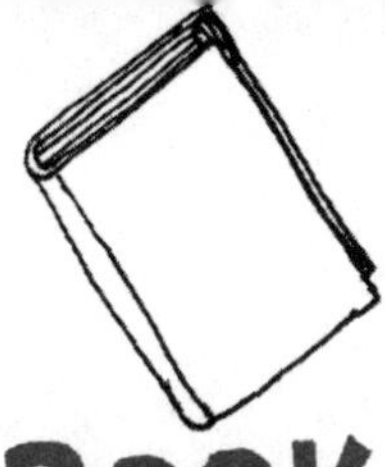

A PART OF A BOOK

LOCATION FOUND: ____________

TIME: ________ DATE: ________

STORY: ______________________

Add something orange.

Combine with an everyday object.

69

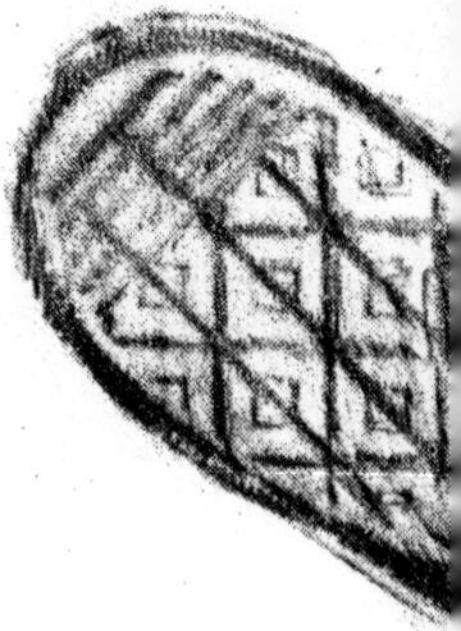

A PENCIL RUBBING OF THE BOTTOM OF A SHOE

LOCATION FOUND: ____________

TIME: ________ DATE: ____________

STORY: ________________________

Do something you never do.

Make it white.

70

SOMETHING FROM A CONSTRUCTION SITE

LOCATION FOUND: ______________

TIME: ________ DATE: ____________

STORY: ______________________

____

____

____

____

____

____

____

____

____

____

Turn it into something else.

Re-create it in another material.

71

50995

9 780671 69688 0

0-671-69588-6

A UPC SYMBOL

LOCATION FOUND: ____________

TIME: ______ DATE: ________

STORY: ______________

Place it into a new environment.

Add an arrow (or a series of arrows).

72

A PIECE OF GREEN FABRIC

LOCATION FOUND: ____________

TIME: ______ DATE: ________

STORY: ______________

Add clouds.

Smudge pencil lines with your finger.

SOME EXTRA THINGS

(FURTHER SCAVENGING)

Trim into new shape.

Trace shapes over top.

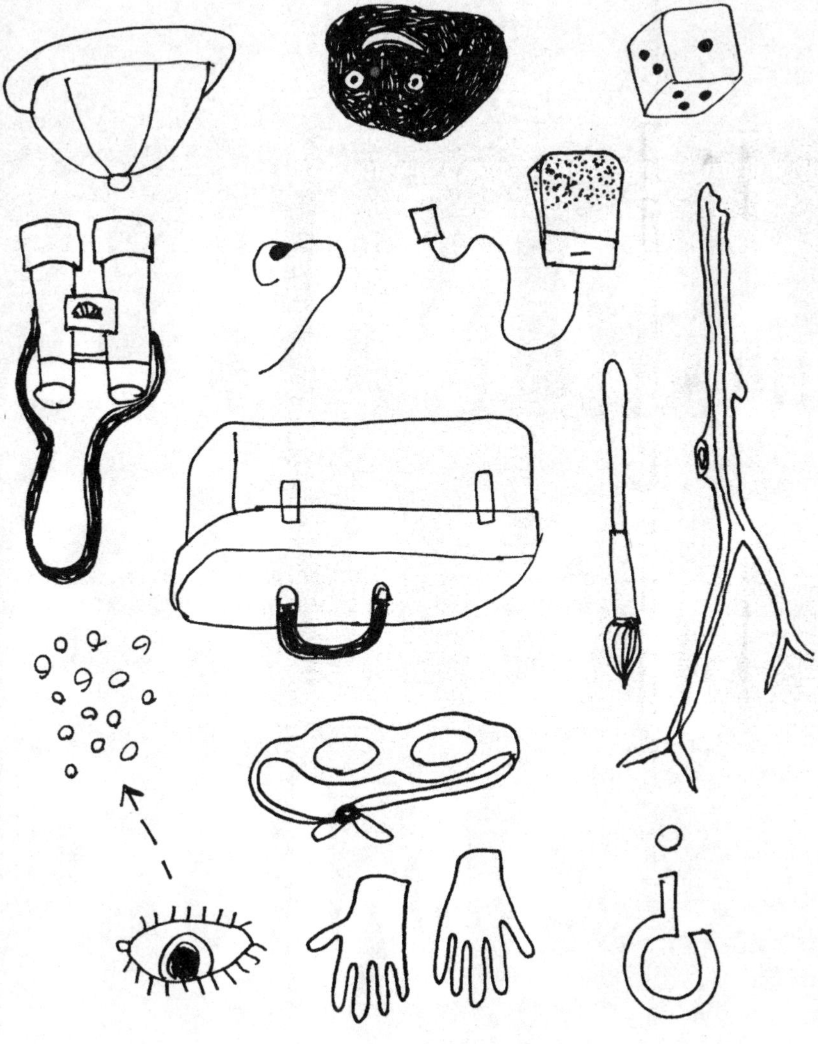

FUN THINGS TO DO

- Play a game with two or more people. Assign an item for everyone to collect. Then have everyone use the same alteration. Impose a time limit for the alteration. Compare results.

- Try doing several alterations to each item. You may wish to roll a die to tell you how many alterations to employ.

- Try completing all of the collecting at once, and then begin the alterations.

- Try collecting multiples of one of the items and experimenting with many different alterations (or combinations of alterations).

- Make an exhibit with your items. Create a mini museum in a public forum.

- Start a scavenger flash mob. Invite people to do a public scavenger hunt on a social network.

- Create your own scavenges. Hide things for a friend to find on their way to school/work.

- Conduct a scavenging workshop, or create a club. Pick a new item to find every week.

- Take the things you have collected and explore them further. Conduct research. Trace the origins. Look at them from many different perspectives, shape, color, texture, history, etc. Pretend you are new to the planet. What do these items tell you about the inhabitants of earth?

- Take your altered items and create some kind of narrative based on them.

- Experiment with the scavenges on the following pages.

Give it an interesting title or caption.

Turn it into a mask.

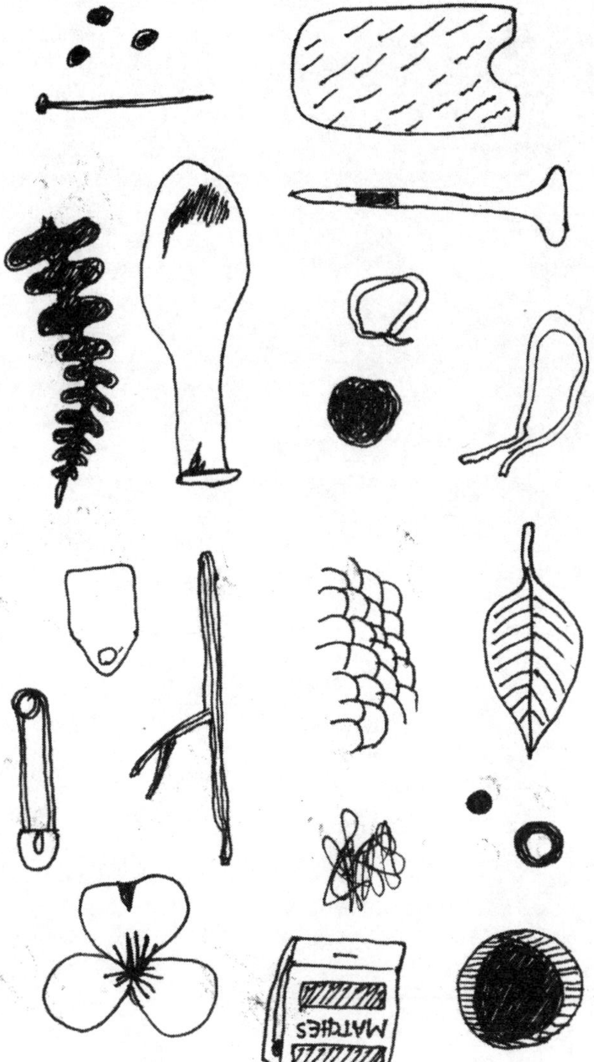

RANDOM SCAVENGE

1. Take a walk in your neighborhood.

2. Collect twenty things you find on your walk.

3. Document them on a map. Write a story about each item.

Add a black shape.

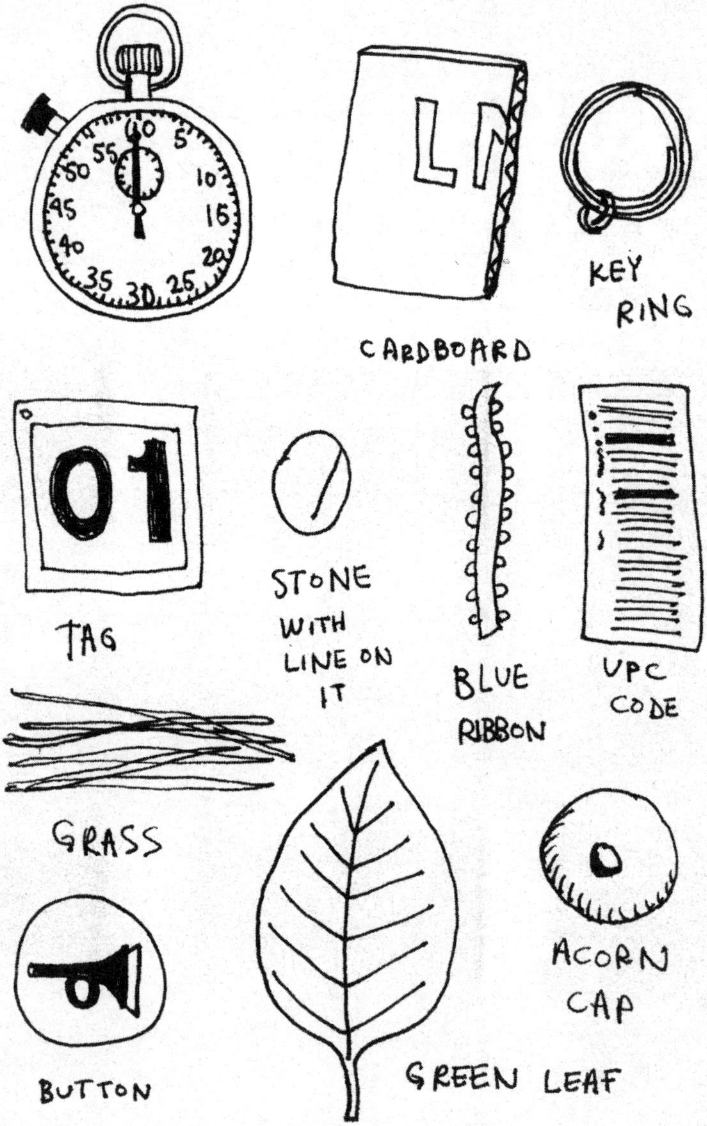

Combine with another object.

QUICK SCAVENGE

Collect ten things in ten minutes.

Tear shapes out of paper to add.

Add a dotted line.

SOUND SCAVENGE

Using some kind of sound recorder, record ten different sounds you hear in your environment.

If you do not have a sound recorder you can make up different symbols for the sounds you hear and mark them on a map or graph.

Add a yellow object.

Add something shiny.

SKETCH SCAVENGE

1. Go for a walk in a predetermined location.

2. Sketch ten items you find.

3. Document the locations on a map.

Add a crooked line.

Add a blob.

ALPHABET SCAVENGE

You must find and document the whole alphabet while out on a walk. You will need to use a camera for this.

Find and add something with a similar shape.

Draw the outline of a tree.

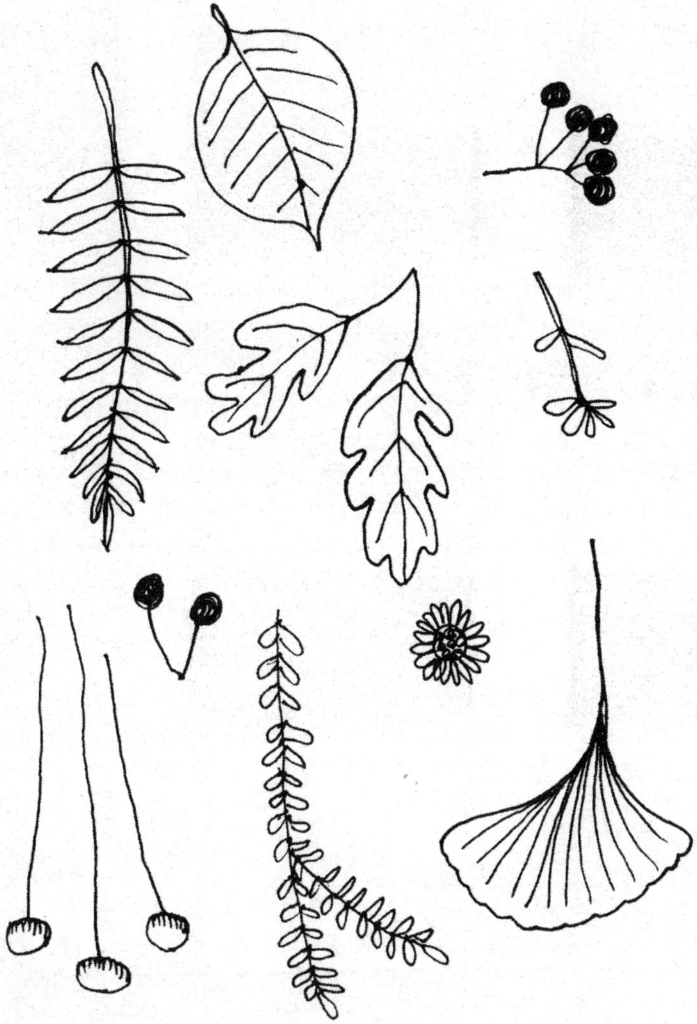

PLANT SCAVENGE

1. Go to a specific outdoor location.

2. Collect as many different kinds of wild plants as you can. (Make sure to avoid poison oak and stinging nettles!) (Note: If it is a place where the flora and fauna are protected, such as a state park, then document with photos.) It may be helpful to use a plant identification guidebook.

3. Arrange your collection and try to identify the plants using a field guide.

Build it up.

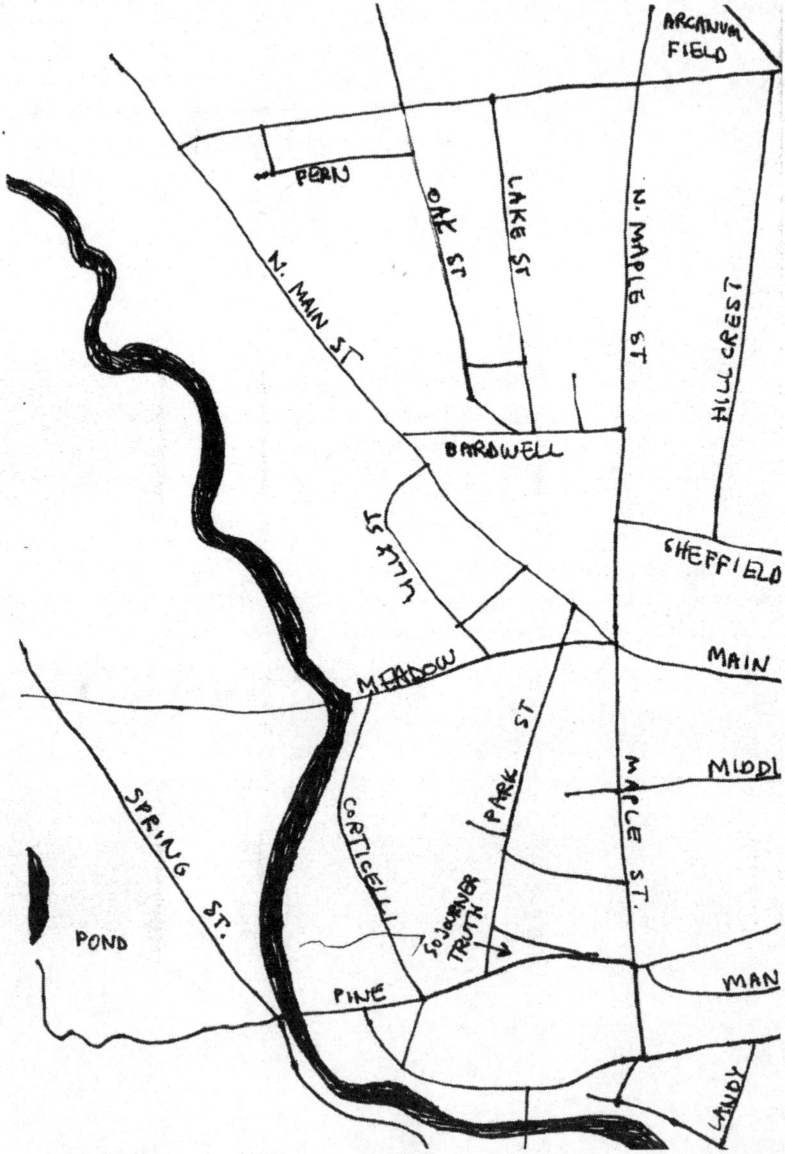

Build it up with layers.

MAP SCAVENGE

1. Choose a specific location with defined boundaries (park, street block).

2. Go for a walk and choose ten objects/landmarks.

3. Create a set of clues for each thing (for example, next to the red fire hydrant, something that is yellow).

4. Give the clues to a friend and have your friend locate each item.

Wild card. Choose an alteration yourself.

Create your own alteration.

STAINS AND SPILLS

Go out and document as many stains or spills as you can. (You could also include discarded gum or shapes made by water.)

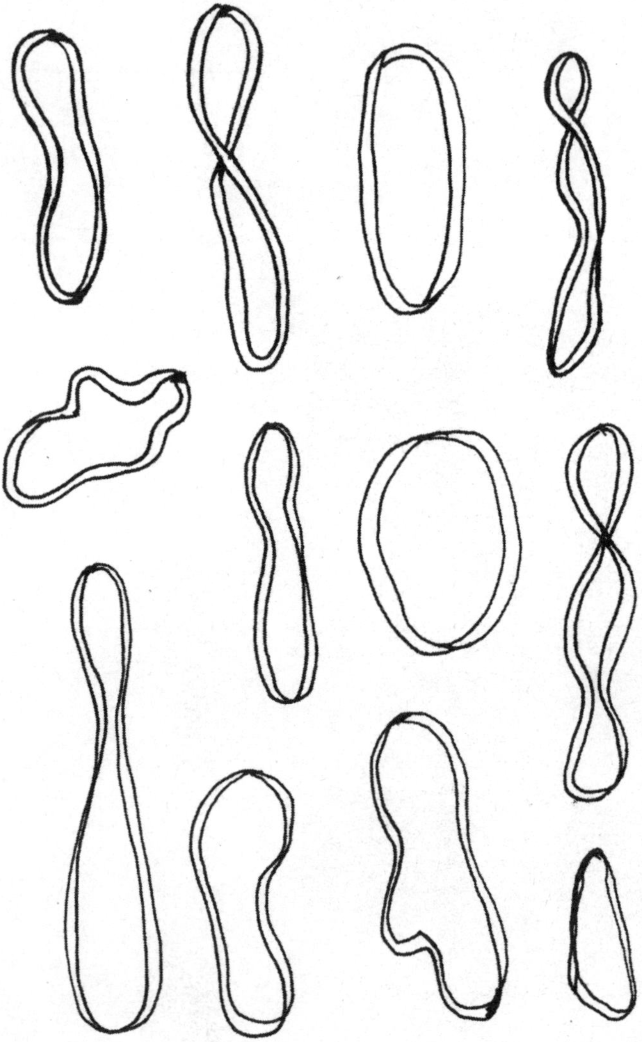

Fill every square inch with something.

ONE THING SCAVENGE

1. Choose one object to collect or document. (Some ideas: blue things, rubber bands, tickets, stamps, park benches, etc.)

2. Look for the object everywhere you go. Collect or document it in some way.

Go crazy on it.

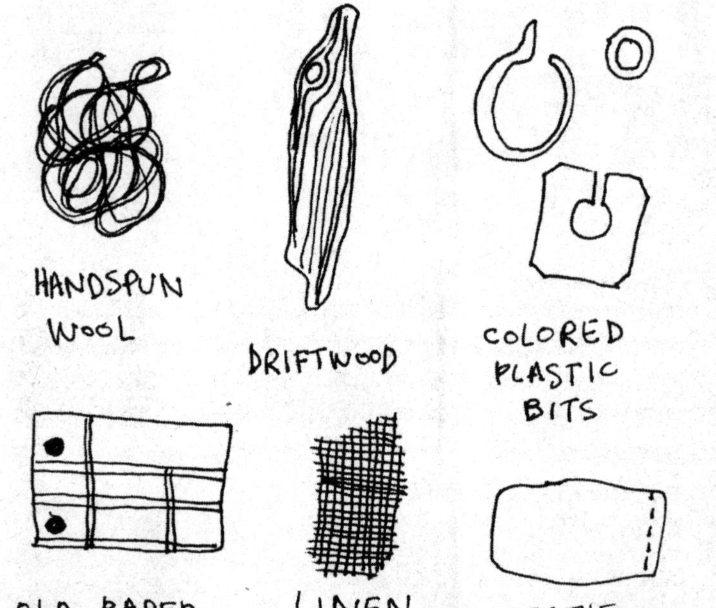

Draw as slowly as humanly possible.

PERSONAL SCAVENGE

1. Create a scavenge based on your own personal preferences and tastes (for example, find a wrapper from your favorite candy, find a variety of textures you really enjoy).

2. Give it to a friend to use.

Go away for five minutes. Come back and doodle somthin

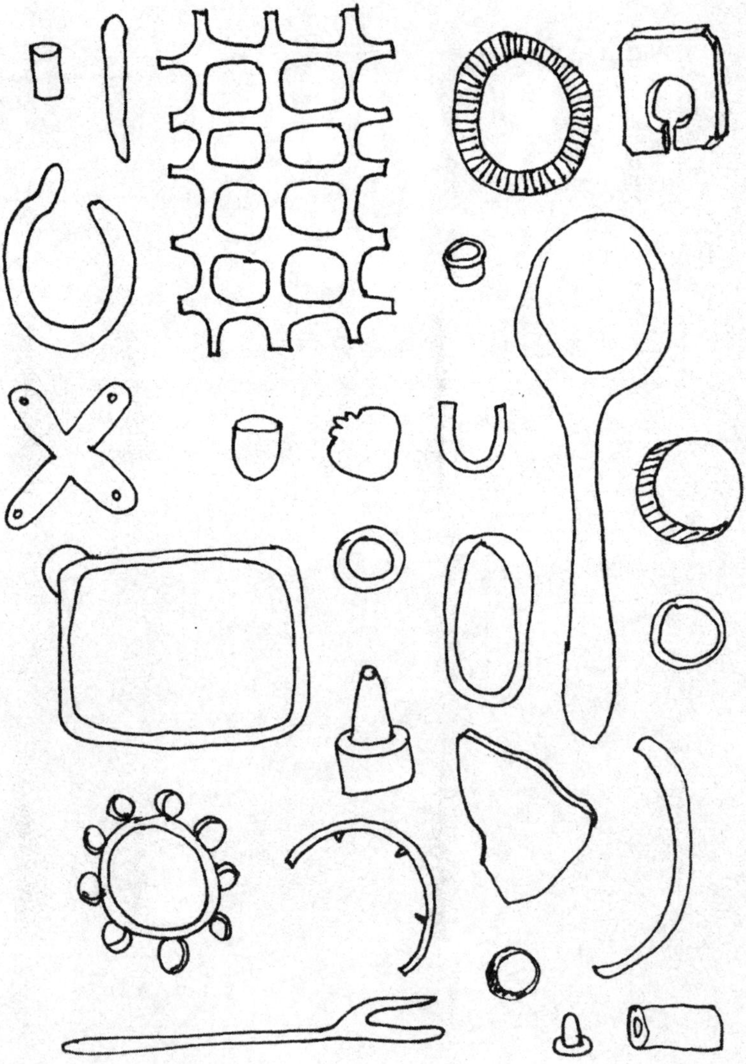

Add as many things as you can.

PLASTIC SCAVENGE

1. Collect as many pieces of discarded plastic as you can.

2. Document them separately or as a group.

3. Create some kind of installation with the pieces.

Make part of it pretty and part of it ugly.

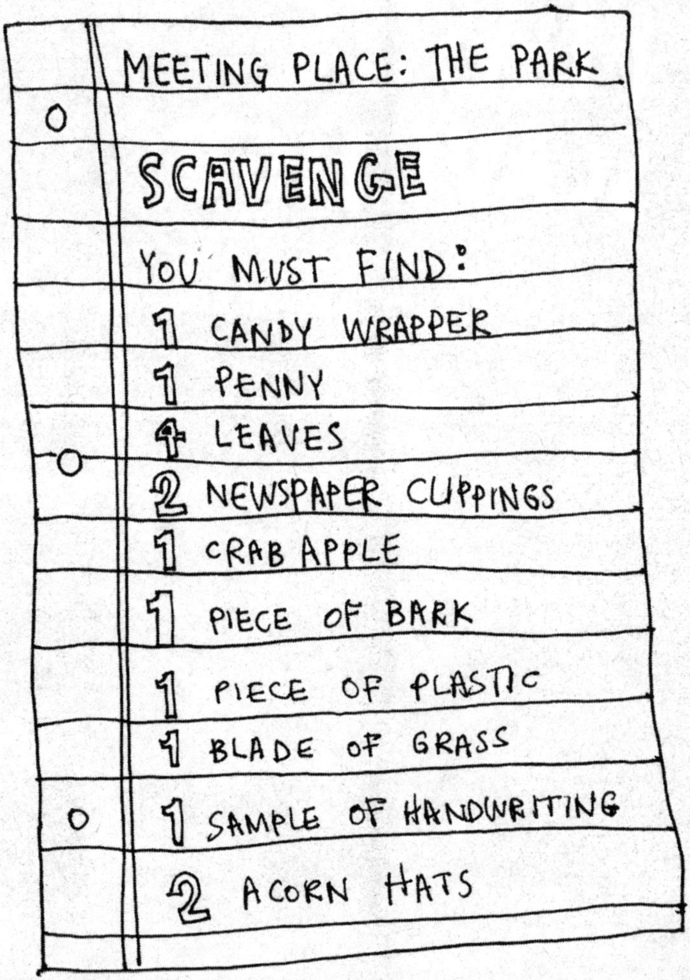
MEETING PLACE: THE PARK
SCAVENGE
YOU MUST FIND:
1 CANDY WRAPPER
1 PENNY
4 LEAVES
2 NEWSPAPER CLIPPINGS
1 CRAB APPLE
1 PIECE OF BARK
1 PIECE OF PLASTIC
1 BLADE OF GRASS
1 SAMPLE OF HANDWRITING
2 ACORN HATS

Assemble some art materials. Use them all.

MEETING SCAVENGE

1. Arrange to meet a friend at a specific location.

2. Each person gives a scavenge assignment to the other to collect a predetermined number of objects.

Preserve it.

Incorporate fruit.

URBAN FOSSILS

Go out and document as many urban fossils as you can find. These will be things that have been embedded somehow in concrete sidewalks—footprints (animal and human), leaf prints, patterns, coins, names, etc.

Photograph it. Include photo.

CHECKLIST

QUICK REFERENCE LIST OF ITEMS

Make a statement.

Turn it into something that flies.

- ☐ POSTAGE STAMPS
- ☐ THE NUMBER FIVE
- ☐ A PAPER CLIP
- ☐ A FEATHER
- ☐ A USED ENVELOPE
- ☐ A TICKET
- ☐ NINE CIRCLES
- ☐ CURRENCY
- ☐ SEE THROUGH
- ☐ THREE DIFFERENT TEXTURES
- ☐ TEXT
- ☐ A POST-IT NOTE
- ☐ A PIECE OF MOSS
- ☐ SOME WIRE
- ☐ SOMETHING YOU ATE
- ☐ LOCAL ENVIRONMENT
- ☐ ON YOUR BODY
- ☐ A USED TEA BAG
- ☐ A NAPKIN
- ☐ SOMETHING STICKY
- ☐ SIX BLUE THINGS
- ☐ PUZZLE PIECE
- ☐ AN ELASTIC BAND
- ☐ CHARACTER
- ☐ SEVERAL LEAVES
- ☐ RED STRING
- ☐ A WRAPPER
- ☐ A PHOTO OF YOURSELF
- ☐ A POSTCARD
- ☐ FOUR SQUARES
- ☐ FIVE BUTTONS
- ☐ ELEPHANT
- ☐ ROCK TRACINGS
- ☐ SOMETHING ORANGE
- ☐ YEAR YOU WERE BORN
- ☐ HANDWRITTEN QUOTE
- ☐ FIVE SAMPLES HANDWRITING
- ☐ GRAVESTONE RUBBING
- ☐ A HAIR SAMPLE
- ☐ FORTUNE
- ☐ COUPON
- ☐ SOMETHING BROKEN
- ☐ SOMETHING DISCARDED
- ☐ LIQUID STAIN
- ☐ GREEN STAIN
- ☐ SOMETHING CRUMBLED
- ☐ SOMETHING DRAGGED
- ☐ PART OF A TREE
- ☐ SOMETHING PLANTED
- ☐ A FOUND NOTE
- ☐ FLAT CANDY
- ☐ SEED PODS
- ☐ LEFT BY AN ANIMAL
- ☐ MACHINE MADE
- ☐ HANDMADE
- ☐ MINIATURE
- ☐ ORIGAMI
- ☐ GIVEN TO YOU
- ☐ DRAWING
- ☐ GRASS
- ☐ IMAGINARY
- ☐ STYROFOAM
- ☐ PLASTIC
- ☐ SPOTS
- ☐ SOMETHING CURVED
- ☐ SIX TRIANGLES
- ☐ HOLE IN IT
- ☐ PART OF A BOOK
- ☐ BOTTOM OF SHOE
- ☐ CONSTRUCTION SITE
- ☐ UPC SYMBOL
- ☐ GREEN FABRIC

What would it say if it could talk?

THIS PAGE IS RESERVED FOR A

MYSTERY OBJECT*

* AN OBJECT YOU FIND WHILE ON A SCAVENGE THAT IS NOT ON THE LIST BUT IS TOO GOOD TO PASS UP.

LOCATION FOUND: ____________

TIME: ______ DATE: ________

STORY: ____________________

Add a paper bag.

BIBLIOGRAPHY

Abram, David. The Spell of the Sensuous. New York: Vintage, 1997.

Bachelard, Gaston. The Poetics of Space. Boston: Beacon Press, 1994.

Buchanan-Smith, Peter. Speck: A Curious Collection of Uncommon Things. New York: Princeton Architectural Press, 2001.

Elpel, Thomas J. Botany in a Day: The Patterns Method of Plant Identification. Pony, Montana: HOPS Press, 2004.

Fletcher, Allan. The Art of Looking Sideways. New York: Phaidon Press, 2001.

Fletcher, Allan. Picturing and Poeting. New York: Phaidon Press, 2006.

Gooley, Tristan. The Natural Navigator. New York: The Experiment, 2010.

Harmon, Katherine. You Are Here: Personal Geographies and Other Maps of the Imagination. New York: Princeton Architectural Press, 2003.

Jernigan, Candy. Evidence: The Art of Candy Jernigan. San Francisco: Chronicle Books, 1999.

Create a collage.

Johnstone, Stephen (editor). The Everyday. Boston: MIT Press, 2008.

Kent, Corita. Learning by Heart. Allworth Press: 2008.

Munari, Bruno. From Afar It Was an Island. Verona, Italy: Corraini, 1971.

Munari, Bruno. The Sea as Craftsman. Mantova Italy, 1995.

Munari, Bruno. The Tactile Workshops. Mantova Italy, 1985.

Perec, Georges. The Species of Spaces and Other Pieces. New York: Penguin, 2008.

Tuan, Yi-Fu. Space and Place: The Perspective of Experience. Boston: Beacon Press, 1994.

Wilde, Ann and Jürgen Wilde (editors). Karl Blossfeldt: Working Collages. Boston: MIT Press, 2001.

Documentary Films

The Gleaners and I by Agnès Varda

Waste Land by Lucy Walker, João Jardim, and Karen Harley

ALSO FROM KERI SMITH

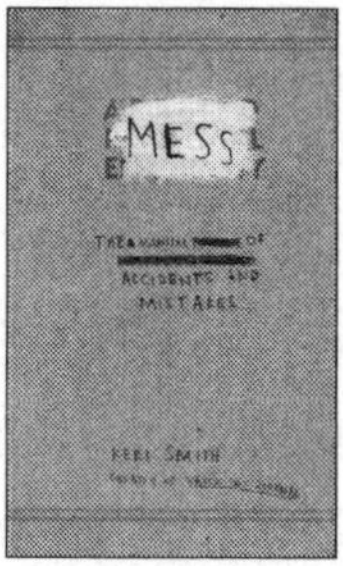

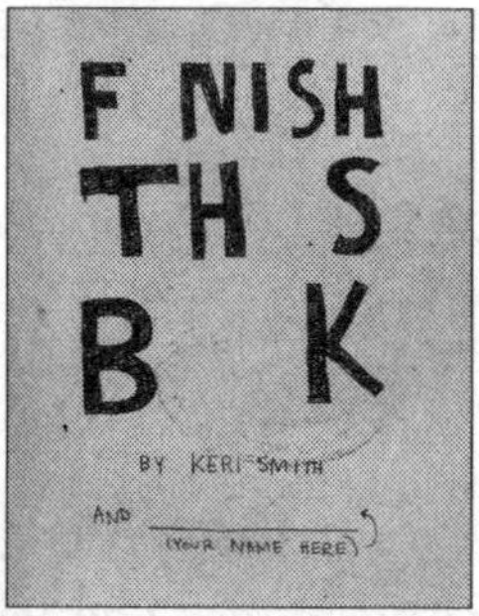

AVAILABLE FOR APPLE AND SUPPORTED ANDROID DEVICES!

PARTICULAR BOOKS
an imprint of
PENGUIN BOOKS

T258-0213

Add the sun.